Touched by Robert Burns

Andy Hall was born in 1954 and was brought up in the north-east of Scotland. He graduated from Aberdeen University with a Bachelor of Education degree in 1977. His study of Scottish literature, particularly that of Lewis Grassic Gibbon and Robert Burns, had a powerful influence on him and shaped his love of the Scottish landscape, encouraging him to convey its essential elements through the medium of photography.

Andy's reputation as a photographer of places and people has gained international recognition as a result of the success of his books, *A Sense of Belonging to Scotland*, *The Favourite Places of Scottish Personalities* and *A Sense of Belonging to Scotland, Further Journeys*. Many examples of his work can be seen on his website *www.asenseofbelonging.com*

TOUCHED BY ROBERT BURNS

Images and Insights

ANDY HALL

Foreword by **Sir Alex Ferguson**

BIRLINN

First published in 2008 by
Birlinn Limited
West Newington House
10 Newington Road
Edinburgh
EH9 1QS

www.birlinn.co.uk

ISBN13: 978 1 84158 688 5

British Library Cataloguing-in-Publication Data
A catalogue record for this book is available from the British Library

Typeset in Adobe Jenson and Gill Sans at Birlinn

Printed and bound in Slovenia

CONTENTS

Foreword by Sir Alex Ferguson ☆ vii

Introduction ☆ ix

FOREWORD
by Sir Alex Ferguson CBE
Manager of Manchester United FC and UNICEF Ambassador

It is with the greatest of pleasure that I write the foreword for this latest work of Andy Hall, *Touched by Robert Burns*. His photography of Scottish subjects has captivated people like me for many years.

As an ambassador for UNICEF, I am also delighted that Andy, through this book, has highlighted the role of UNICEF in tackling the worldwide problems of children who are subjected to poverty, exploitation and lack of education.

I am sure that all who are avid readers of Robert Burns would endorse the view that the great bard himself would have supported such a worthy cause. Although most of his work as a young boy was not nearly as arduous as that which we know is done by children in other parts of the world, nonetheless his frugal upbringing as a boy, working on the farm and then off to school, was certainly a huge burden for him to carry.

Having read most of his poems, I marvel at Burns' ability to transfer his observations of life into poems or songs and onto paper. Let's be honest, most of us jump when we see a mouse, but not, it seems, Burns. He studied the mouse he came across in a field and put his thoughts into his famous poem.

All Scots are rightly proud of the Ayrshire Bard. His works are world renowned and he is recognized everywhere. A good question to consider is how many Burns Nights are held in the entire world? I myself know of some friends who go to the annual Burns Supper in Moscow!

I look forward to this latest publication by Andy Hall. I know how meticulous he is in his work and I wish him well.

Alex Ferguson

Sir Alex Ferguson CBE

INTRODUCTION

Robert Burns was born on the 25th of January, 1759, at Alloway in Ayrshire, and died on the 21st of July, 1796, at Dumfries. He was only 37 years of age at the time of his death.

His father, William, was a farmer from a few miles south of Stonehaven in Kincardineshire in the north east of Scotland. William held education and the value of humankind in high regard. His greatest gift to his son, Robert, was to pass on these values.

As well as having great importance put on his education, embedded in Robert were an innate sensitivity and an ability to choose and use the language of poetry to distil the most fundamental aspects of the human condition.

To put it at its simplest, he was a genius who expressed himself in poetry, but to describe him in these terms does not explain why his works are celebrated every January throughout the world. His poems have a timeless relevance to people of all nationalities. Despite having a struggling and restricted life in eighteenth-century Scotland, his understanding of humanity, its intellect and its soul, has made his poetry universal. The nature of man, woman and the delicate workings of the natural world are revealed throughout his poems.

Though he was born into a poor environment, Robert Burns created a huge canon of works of literary and academic significance while, at the same time, being able to touch the soul of the common man. Therein lies his genius.

The life and works of Burns have been studied and documented in universities throughout the world. This collection of images and insights is not an academic analysis of his poetry. It is an attempt to convey in short articles or in a single image the real meaning of Robert Burns, 250 years after his birth. Because my genre and passion is photography, I set myself the challenge of interpreting words, lines and verses from his poetry through that visual medium.

When I conceived of the idea for this publication, it was the lightness of touch of Burns' writing and everyday presence of his influence that intrigued me. I am delighted that so many people have been willing to embrace this opportunity of expressing their thoughts and feelings about Scotland's universal bard.

The images and insights in this collection are intimate expressions of the ways in which Burns's words resonate with the contributors and myself. I hope they act as a catalyst for people to take a moment to reflect on what it means for them, too, to be touched by Robert Burns.

In the spirit of the poet's feelings about human rights, justice, fairness and compassion, all royalties from this publication are in aid of UNICEF.

Andy Hall

Dedication

I would like to dedicate this book to my friend Alfie Smith, whose love of Robert Burns is reflected in his 55-year membership of the Stonehaven (Fatherland) Burns Club.

Touched by Robert Burns

Seamus Heaney

Nobel Prizewinner for Literature

A Birl for Burns

From the start, Burns' birl and rhythm,
That tongue the Ulster Scots brought with them
And stick to still in County Antrim
       Was in my ear.
From east of Bann it westered in
       On the Derry air.

My neighbours *toved* and *bummed* and *blowed*,
They *happed* themselves until it *thowed*.
By *slaps* and *stiles* they *thrawed* and *tholed*
       And *snedded thrissles,*
And when the rigs were *braked* and *hoed*
       They'd *wet their whistles.*

Old men and women getting crabbed
Would hark like dogs who'd seen a rabbit,
Then straighten, stare and have a stab at
       Standard habbie:
Custom never staled their habit
       O' quotin' Rabbie.

Leg-lifting, heartsome, lightsome Burns!
He overflowed the well-wrought urns
Like buttermilk from slurping churns,
       Rich and unruly,
Or dancers flying, doing turns
       At some wild hooley.

For Rabbie's free and Rabbie's big.
His stanza may be tight and trig
But once he sets sail and rig,
       Away he goes
Like Tam o' Shanter o'er the brig
       Where no one follows.

And though his first tongue's going, gone,
And word lists now get added on
And even words like *stroan* and *thrawn*
       Have to be glossed,
In Burns's rhymes they travel on
       And won't be lost.

Burns Cottage, Alloway, Ayrshire
Where Robert Burns was born on 25 January, 1759.

Rt. Hon. Alex Salmond

Scotland's First Minister

Robert Burns deserves the high regard in which he is held both at home and worldwide. He restored to Scots a pride in their country and culture, battered as that had been in the years following the Union contrived by the 'parcel o' rogues'.

Burns celebrated our countryside and our folkways, and satirised, mercilessly, the pretensions and hypocrisies to which we are all given, though few on the grand scale of Holy Willie. He either wrote or rescued from oblivion some of the finest love songs in the world, and he set in its classical form the worldwide hymn to friendship and the memory of good times past that is 'Auld Lang Syne'. He wrote the great comic epic of *Tam o' Shanter*. He celebrated the brotherhood and sisterhood of all human beings, and showed that proper national pride goes hand in hand with a reverence for universal humanity.

My favourite Burns verse of all is from 'A Man's a Man for A' That'. It is the one that expresses his deep-held regard for democratic equality and independence of mind:

> Ye see yon birkie ca'd 'a lord',
>   Wha struts, an' stares, and a' that?
> Tho hundreds worship at his word,
>   He's but a cuif for a' that.
> For a' that, an a' that,
>   His ribband, star, an a' that,
> The man o independent mind,
>   He looks an laughs at a' that.

It is indeed from thoughts like these that auld Scotia's grandeur springs, and I try to act in their spirit in all that I do.

Then let us pray that come it may,
(As come it will for a' that),
That Sense and Worth o'er a' the earth
Shall bear the gree an a' that.
For a' that, an a' that,
It's comin yet for a' that,
That man to man, the world o'er,
Shall brithers be for a' that.

A Man's a Man for A' That

Dr Maya Angelou

Writer and Academic

I remember thirsting for more understanding when I read my first Robert Burns poem. I, like everyone else, sang 'Auld Lang Syne' as part of the New Year celebration. When I told my brother Bailey, who was two years my senior, and who knew everything, that I could not understand the poem, he said that Robert Burns only wrote some English much as Paul Laurence Dunbar used English to write his black dialect poems.

Bailey dared me to compete with him. The contest would show who could most quickly translate a Burns poem. Using 'Auld Lang Syne' as an example, I worked out 'A Man's a Man for A' That'. I invented words for those I could not translate. When Bailey read the poem translated into contemporary English, he said since the theme of the poem was men and since he was a man, it was fitting that he take my poem and that I should find another.

We both loved each Burns poem I translated until I reached 'Poor Mailie's Elegy', which I loved and claimed for myself. In my youth, I decided Robert Burns had written that poem with a lonely southern black girl in mind.

He became as important to me as Dunbar, Countee Cullen, Langston Hughes and Shakespeare. And today, more than fifty years later, he remains among my favorite poets.

We twa hae paidl'd in the burn
Frae morning sun till dine,
But seas between us braid hae roar'd
Sin auld lang syne.

Auld Lang Syne

John Cairney

Actor, Writer, Lecturer and Painter

In 1959, I was on track to make it as a classical actor, being offered a chance to join the Old Vic and later the newly-formed Royal Shakespeare Company after successful seasons at the Glasgow Citizens' Theatre and the Bristol Old Vic. Instead, a poster on Paddington Station showing Burns surrounded by characters from his life and works gave me the idea of a theatrical one-man show. This not only diverted my career onto another line but also altered the destination of my whole life from then on. It was if a hand had reached out from the poster and pointed the way.

I was then working mainly in films and television and wasn't free to put the idea into practice until 1965, by which time Tom Wright had written a solo play at my suggestion, and *There Was a Man* was produced by Gerard Slevin at the tiny Traverse Theatre in Edinburgh on 25 January, 1965.

Jim Haynes, the Yank at the Traverse, decided to take the risk on one man and Burns, and offered a trial week at the Traverse at a pound a night. The gamble came off. I was invited to take the show to London's West End and from there it went to the Geneva Festival and eventually to the United States, Canada, Australia, New Zealand and South Africa – even to Russia and on round-the-world cruises – over the next forty years. Ironically, when I first touted the solo idea, Gerry Slevin had said to me, 'You know if this comes off, you could be playing it till you're forty.' I played him until I was 75.

I never tired of it, because I never tired of Burns. His international appeal was inexhaustible and audiences proved that, whether they were in the largest theatre, the smallest back room or swishest hotel restaurant. I played him in every possible kind of venue to all sorts of people and the result at the end was always the same – a beautiful silence. This is the best kind of applause an actor can get, but it was Robert Burns who earned it. Which is why, whenever I get the chance, I go to Dumfries and lay a red rose on the doorstep of the house where he died at exactly half the age I am now.

The man opened so many doors for me. And if he did indeed touch me from that Paddington poster all those years ago, I am proud to say that I have been able in my time, through his lines, to touch others in playing him for a fee in the theatre – and not for a pound a night. The truth is it was nothing to do with money or careerism. Indeed, from a career point of view, it was a great mistake. It was a heart matter and I followed it unhesitatingly. This is something I shall never regret. I will never lose touch with Burns, because he has never yet failed to touch me.

Our monarch's hindmost year but ane
Was five-and-twenty days begun,
'Twas then a blast o' Janwar' Win'
Blew Hansel in on Robin.

There Was a Lad

Eddi Reader

Singer and Songwriter

My exploration of Rab Mossgiel was due, in part, to the Ayrshire writer of the song 'Wild Mountainside', John Douglas of the Trashcan Sinatras, *'only a mile to go ...'*

The first time I met that song, I was living in London feeling homesick and needing to be nearer my culture, therefore closer to my roots and family. John wrote it as a request for me to make the journey home.

My father's death at the age of 60 with asbestos poisoning happened just before I heard that song. My years seemed to be getting shorter and to be home became a burning desire for me after running far and fast away 22 years earlier.

In the same year, I was asked by the Royal Scottish National Orchestra to join with them in celebrating the work of Robert Burns. I was to sing three Burns songs in the garden of Culzean Castle in Ayr with them one day in May. This led to one of the biggest love affairs of my life, and I began exploring every bit of Burns history that I could find.

I became a bit obsessed; I began to see my dad in Robert Burns' Scottish humour. Robert seemed as much 'home' to me as my own family. He allowed me to fall in love with Scottish masculinity, and I could see quite clearly, for the first time perhaps, a real connection to my own culture. I hadn't thought about it much before that time, but I began to feel I was missing even more than missing my father – I was missing experiencing my own life!

Celtic Connections festival asked me to repeat and expand my performance of Burns' work with the orchestra. They booked me to do a fuller set of Robert Burns' music over two nights at the Concert Hall in Glasgow. So, with the songs of Robert Burns guiding me across the Border and the song 'Wild Mountainside' encouraging my heart, I left my London life behind me, came home, recorded an album of Robert's songs and included the 'new' Ayrshire song of John Douglas.

I am like a newborn puppy in the middle of my brood. God bless Scotland!

Wee, modest, crimson-tipped flow'r,
Thou's met me in an evil hour;
For I maun crush amang the stoure
Thy slender stem:
To spare thee now is past my pow'r,
Thou bonie gem.

To a Mountain Daisy. *On turning one down with the plough, in April 1786*

Phil Cunningham

Musician and Musical Producer

Until a few days ago, I was pretty sure I knew what Robert Burns meant to me. I knew that at primary school, we were not allowed to speak Scots unless we were reciting or singing Burns (albeit with perfectly rounded vowels.) The annual school competition brought great excitement as we all battled for the coveted Burns prize, once mine for 'To a Mouse'.

His songs were, I suppose, my first introduction to 'traditional music'. Over the years I have struggled with arranging and rearranging his songs for gigs, albums and television performances, I've marvelled at each new thing I learned whilst presenting TV programmes about him, perused countless glossaries as I strained to understand him… I'm currently on my sixteenth arrangement of 'Auld Lang Syne' for Hogmanay (one of them sung by Basil Brush!) and I'm constantly seeking new ways to present him to the wider public.

I try to celebrate his birthday without fail every year, no matter where I am in the world. One year in Germany, and finding a haggis somewhat hard to come by, my pals and I ended up piping in a rolled-up kilt sock on a 'borrowed' silver platter, reciting 'Address to a Haggis', stabbing the sock at the appropriate point, and having a few toasts and a dram or two nonetheless. I roared with laughter as an old pal recounted a Scots-German-English translation of 'To a Haggis' he had heard on his travels:

> 'A blessing on your honest ruddy countenance,
> Great fuehrer of the sausage people!'

I have played penny whistle to accompany an aged Japanese couple who sang 'Auld Lang Syne' to me on an Inverness-Edinburgh train, an act which formed the basis of a very unexpected friendship.

Burns's poetry has inspired me to read the poetry of others. I persuaded my sister and her husband to use Burns to renew their marriage vows. I'm sure you are beginning to get the picture. He has been such a constant part of my life that perhaps I have been taking him a wee bit for granted.

Then, on the 31st of May 2007, I found myself deep beneath the National Library of Scotland holding a letter. *The* very letter he had sent to his dear 'Clarinda'. On that page, he had written the words to 'Ae Fond Kiss', with his handwriting, his own urgency to reach her before she left for Jamaica, his own suggestion for his preferred tune for the song.

Suddenly it was all too much for me. I was close to tears, dumbstruck, overawed . . . all of the above! It would appear . . . that I have greatly underestimated what Robert Burns means to me.

Fair fa' his honest sonsie face!

Plaque over the grave of 'Clarinda' (Agnes McLehose)
in Canongate Kirkyard, Edinburgh

Sir Alex Ferguson

Manager of Manchester United FC, UNICEF Ambassador

I, like many Scottish people, didn't appreciate the values that Robbie Burns set down as a great Scotsman, simply because we never got it at school. Now that is a crime, considering that Scottish education in those times was recognised as one of the best in the world.

However, in my late teens, I was travelling with some friends in the north side of Glasgow one day when the subject of Burns came up, and although aware of this great poet, I was not versed enough in his work to enter the debate. Anyway, the view that provoked most anger from one of my friends, Walter Glen, was that Burns died a young man chiefly through his womanising.

Well, Walter, who was a great aficionado of Burns, tore that theory to shreds, and then enlightened us on the real Robbie Burns. He reminded us that, coming from a farming family, it was extremely unlikely that he or his brother Gilbert were allowed any great amount of freedom to be habitual drinkers or womanisers. No, he had to work that farm for long hours. It was here that he got the inspiration for many of his works, 'To a Mouse' for example.

Close examination tells us clearly of a different and special man with a great social conscience, particularly about Scottish interests, and keen to put it into verse. 'A Man's a Man for A' That' is recognised as one of the world's most influential poems in reminding us of our worth and humility and honesty. I know when thinking of Burns and trying to grasp where he got his inspiration, imagination and drive from, it reminds me of myself in times when I feel I need to escape and think. Sometimes I go into a sort of cocoon. I am happy in there and can think and clear my head.

At the height of his powers in 1787 he went on three different tours – the first with Robert Ainslie to the Borders for three weeks, the second, again for three weeks, to the Highlands and lastly with Dr Adair to Stirlingshire, and I wonder if that was where he got thinking time for his work or just to clear his head, but when you consider the transport of the day, then it was quite a journey.

I am glad I learned more about Robbie Burns and I'm now able to crystallize his life accurately, a hardworking genius who latterly combined working a farm in Dumfries with travelling 200 miles a week as an exciseman. When you read his works, you realise that in every one of his poems there is a message for us as human beings.

Last year, my local hotel had a Burns Night Dinner and asked me to say something or recite one of his poems; but I am not confident enough to recite, particularly in a room full of English people, but I did talk about his life and achievements. After the dinner it was amazing the number of people who came up to me and said they didn't realise what Burns was really about, and were amazed at how much he crammed into his short life.

So it is fair to say that maybe the Burns story is just starting, as there are more celebrations each January and more insight and study into his life, like that which I, myself, am doing at present.

Mossgiel, near Mauchline, Ayrshire
where Robert and his brother Gilbert farmed from 1784 to 1786

Alexander McCall Smith

Novelist

The first Burns poem that I remember reading as a young boy was 'A Man's a Man for A' That'. It is unusual, I think, to remember the first time one read something as a child – normally the reading of childhood fades into a general blur.

As a boy, I loved Kipling's 'Rikki Tikki Tavi' and could recite it more or less word for word, but I do not remember when I first read it. With Burns, though, I remember the exact moment. And the reason why I remember it is that I remember being moved in a way which I had never before been moved. It was an emotional reaction sufficiently powerful to survive over fifty years of subsequent life.

In my teenage years I think that I read some Burns, but not a great deal. At that stage I had discovered Eliot and, oddly enough, English translations of Yevtushenko. I thought myself tremendously sophisticated to be reading Yevtushenko – teenagers can be real intellectual snobs – and Burns would have been consigned in my imagination to the vaguely folksy, along with the screeds of Longfellow and Wordsworth we were obliged to learn by heart. How wrong one can be at fifteen?

At university, I started to attend Burns Suppers and began to develop a mature understanding of his importance by listening to a number of very well delivered and thoughtful Immortal Memories. That was the point at which I discovered, too, the sublime beauty of the songs. I began to appreciate the way in which Burns's music complemented the sentiments of the words in a particularly unstrained way. 'John Anderson My Jo' struck me as being one of the most beautiful odes to friendship in any poetic tradition. The fact that it expresses the feelings of a woman for a man does not limit it to such relationships; its lines speak to any friendship based on shared experiences and the feelings that come with long familiarity.

I never engaged in any real Burns scholarship, but I still developed a relationship with the poet which is very different from that which I have with other writers (with the exception of Auden). The sheer, electrifying humanity of Burns's work is, I think, the quality which makes it transcend the barriers of time. And this humanity leads us to see him as a friend whose presence with us is vivid and immediate, somebody whom we actually *miss*.

That is perhaps a rather odd thing to say, but I think that it is what many people feel when they contemplate a beloved artist who may have lived a long time ago, whom they never actually knew. We miss such people, in the way in which we miss the dead whom we actually knew. That is why Burns Suppers can become emotional occasions, even if they avoid the maudlin.

Burns is very real to us – we can picture him – and we feel that we are linked with him in friendship and love. We miss him.

The Robin cam to the wren's nest
And keekit in and keekit in,
O weel's me on your auld pow,
Wad ye be in, wad ye be in.

The Wren's Nest

Midge Ure

Musician and Patron of Burnsong

Over the last few years of my life, I have been fortunate enough to be surrounded by so-called symbols of success – gold and platinum albums, honorary degrees from universities that, under normal circumstances, would never have allowed an outstanding academic under-achiever such as myself to darken their doorsteps, the odd Grammy, Nordoff Robbins and Ivor Novello awards and even a 'gong' from the Queen, which I must confess I can't bring myself to use. But the first of these accolades came many years before long trousers were even on the horizon.

Back in the early 1960s, my school in Cambuslang, on the outskirts of Glasgow, held a competition for the singing of Burns songs. Burns and his work are part of the staple, educational diet in Scotland. Being only good at art and music, I saw this as an opportunity to shine in front of the girls in my class as opposed to constantly proving to all and sundry that my Victorianesque teacher was correct and that I was indeed effeminate (trying to grow a Beatle fringe), was completely thick (she may have had a point there) and was destined to become a waste of space and a burden on society in general.

Having entered the aforesaid competition with my rendition of Burns' 'My Love is Like a Red, Red Rose' where I hit notes high enough to send large rabid dogs scurrying for sanctuary, or at least Aled Jones whimpering back to the hills, I found myself on the receiving end of a certificate for the excellence of singing Burns songs. The sense of pride bursting out of 24 Park Street was almost volcanic, and probably, without realizing it at the time, it gave me a taste of what was to unfold in the years to come.

The musical and lyrical imagery of Burns' work stays with you forever once you have been exposed to it. There is no doubt in my mind that the music and poetry taught to me as a child has lived on, and has infiltrated and manifested itself in the work I do.

Little did I know then that, all these years later, I would be the first patron of Burnsong and therefore a classic example of one truly being *Touched by Robert Burns*.

No more a winding the course of yon river,
And marking sweet flowerets so fair;
No more I trace the light footsteps of Pleasure,
But Sorrow and sad-sighing Care.

Where Are the Joys

Sir Ludovic Kennedy

Writer and Broadcaster

Like any good Edinburgh-born Scot, I was introduced to Rabbie Burns early, and he and his verses have been with me all my life. I have forgotten the numerous occasions when, at the close of an evening's *ceilidh* or assembly in the company of a partner he often called 'a winsome lassie', I would try (and usually fail) to recall the words of *all* the verses of 'Auld Lang Syne' – literally Old Long Since, but here a shorthand for recalling and celebrating the days of one's youth.

When I was about eight or nine, my mother gave me a, by now, well-thumbed copy of the Collected Poems which has been a close companion on many of my travels and which runs to just over 700 pages. When my darling wife Moira and I gave poetry recitals up and down the country, we invariably included several of his best known ones.

His output was both varied and prolific, a few famous verses castigating the Scottish parliament for betraying the Scottish people by countersigning the union of the English and Scottish parliaments in 1707 ('Such a parcel of rogues in a nation'), others, like 'To a Mouse', with its memorable lines 'The best-laid schemes o' mice an' men/Gang aft agley' which John Steinbeck appropriated for the title of one of his novels, and 'To a Louse' ('On seeing one on a lady's bonnet at church').

As one scholar who has written perceptively about him said, 'Everyone knew their place and Burns was supposed to know his, but the rightful place he knew to be his was not that which was his birthright.' It was something much more, as he himself readily acknowledged in his 'Lines on meeting with Lord Daer', where in the first verse he shows he has the capacity for self deprecation:

> This wot ye all whom it concerns,
> I, rhymer Rab, alias BURNS,
> > October twenty-third,
> A ne'er to be forgotten day!
> Sae far I sprachl'd up the brae,
> > I dinner'd wi' a Lord.

And by the time he reached the eighth and last verse he knew that he and Daer were equal:

Then from his Lordship I shall learn,
Henceforth to meet with unconcern,
  One rank as well's another;
Nae honest, worthy man need care,
To meet wi' noble, youthfu' Daer,
  For he but meets a brother.

Above all Burns was a poet of the humanities and no one has ever bettered his great love song, 'A Red, Red Rose'.

The Burns Monument in Alloway, Ayrshire

Completed in 1823 to a design by Thomas Hamilton in a Grecian style, the monument was financed by public subscription and was the first monument to honour Robert Burns, Scotland's National Bard.

Dougie MacLean

Singer/Songwriter

I can't remember when I was first aware of Robert Burns ... his poems and songs were just always there! My Mum and Dad and others in my childhood sang his songs and read out the odd poem. There seemed to be a Burns song for every important occasion or celebration, but I never really liked the way his songs were treated – still in a kind of Victorian parlour style that never rang true with me.

It was only once I started to write (and perform) songs myself that I realised what an amazing writer he is. Through arranging songs like 'Green Grow the Rashes' and 'Ye Banks and Braes' in a way that I could enjoy singing them, I found myself getting to the heart of something very special. My own rural upbringing meant I could easily and naturally feel his love of the countryside. But I wondered how a man at that time could capture the voice of the yearning captive as he did in 'A Slave's Lament', how he could so deeply stir the patriotic spirit (as he still does) with his 'Scots Wha' Hae' or our belief in fairness in 'For A' That'. Then there's the great sense of humour that comes through in other poems and songs. Such richness!

Whenever I have the time to delve into it, I'm always aware of the very real human being behind the writing of Robert Burns. He never seems to put the words together merely as an intellectual exercise, there's always a passion and an honesty that resonates through them. He is somehow equally comfortable with hard-hitting and personal political comment (often very outspoken for the time) and with romantic, sentimental human emotion (before 'sentimental' became a dirty word!).

These songs and poems, written from his life's experience or empathetic observation, have a power that timelessly transcends our modern music industry and poetry awards. Burns writes from a genuine place that contains a kind of magic that touches and moves us in ways that I don't think we quite understand ... and maybe shouldn't. I'm inspired and moved by his songs and poems, and when confused about the modern self-conscious attitude to this art, I return to his work and I am reassured.

Wha for Scotland's King and Law
Freedom's sword will strongly draw,
Freeman stand, or Freeman fa',
Let him follow me!

Scots Wha Hae

Eileen McCallum

Actress

As the daughter of two Aberdonian academics who had settled, reluctantly, in the west, I must confess I grew up not 'reckoning' Burns much. Children's verse-speaking competitions had me spouting 'The Puddock', and I loved nothing better than to join my Dad in a bothy ballad or two.

Later, always a voracious reader, I remember devouring James Barke's novels about Burns the man, but soon Grassic Gibbon had grabbed my heart, and hasn't let it go to this day. At my all-girl grammar school, the annual Burns Supper was one of the few occasions to meet boys, and so I'm ashamed to say my attention was never focused on the words of the Bard, whose poems were anyway being delivered *sans* passion but heavy on elocution, while shrill sopranos and constipated tenors murdered the songs.

The turning point – for there was one – came through my folk-music phase in the mid-fifties. One evening I heard 'For the Sake o' Somebody' being sung unaccompanied and with a sweet untrained simplicity, and was 'hooked'. I still love it. That opened a door for me, and I rushed through to discover a treasure-trove of talent.

At the drop of a hat, I sang Burns songs to a small guitar at student parties, though I doubt anyone could hear me, come to think of it, and in an early TV production on BBC Scotland I played the young Jean Armour, and laughed and cried with her.

I've penned many a 'Reply to the Lasses' in my time, and, for examples of Burns's work to include in these, I always chose from the poems and lyrics he wrote from a *woman's* viewpoint. I soon realised that, far from being the selfish philanderer some people condemn, he understood the female psyche very well indeed. From the little tease in 'I'm o'er young to marry yet' and the rueful teenage mother-to-be in 'O wha ma babie-clouts will buy?' to the sexually confident bisom of 'Last May a braw wooer' and the heartbroken young woman wandering the 'banks and braes', he seems to see into our souls.

And not only the young ones held his interest. The definitely-over-the-hill but still game camp-follower of 'My sodger laddie' delights him as much as the solitary but happy 'Bessy with her spinning wheel', and everyone envies the sublimely contented old Mrs John Anderson – or *was* she?

Some years ago I was introduced to the bawdy Burns version of that old favourite – in fact I sang it nightly in a one-woman show at the Edinburgh Fringe. The only verse I can quote here goes:

> I'm backit like a salmon,
>   I'm brestit like a swan,
> My wame it is down-cod,
>   My middle ye may span,
> Frae my tap-knot to ma tae, John,
>   I'm like the new fa'n snow
> And it's a' for your conveniency,
>   John Anderson, my jo.

You'll get the drift. I still smile when I think about – yes, and recognise only too well – the inappropriate frustration of the elderly Mrs. A.!

All my adult life I've walked beside these women. I've linked arms and laughed with the lassies, and tottered doon the brae with the auld yins. They've been my friends from adolescence to senility – and beyond? Oh, I do hope so, girls, because I'd fairly miss you all.

Of a' the airts the wind can blaw,
I dearly like the west,
For there the bonie lassie lives,
The lassie I lo'e best.
There wild woods grow, and rivers row
And monie a hill between,
But day and night my fancy's flight
Is ever wi my Jean

Of A' the Airts

Dr Tom Sutherland

Academic (USA); Former Beirut Hostage

It was midsummer of 1946, and the Second World War was behind us. Coming home from a football game, I had arrived at the bus stop and walked to the end of the McGregor Farm road, across from Stonehouse Farm, where I met Frankie McGregor. We talked, and all of a sudden he asked, 'Have you studied any Burns poetry yet?'

'No,' I said, 'but I think next year in my fourth year at Grangemouth High with Miss McEwan...'

'Well,' said Frankie, 'I want you to have this volume of Burns's poems.'

Amazed at his generosity, I took the book home and opened it – a volume published by Collins of London and Glasgow, entitled *Burns Poetical Works*, and there it began. I still have it in my library, the binding now worn out, the pages dog-eared, but precious to me as my first book of Burns. And it has gone with me everywhere, to Glasgow University, to Reading University, to Iowa State University and graduate school, to Colorado State University where I taught for twenty-five years, and ultimately to Beirut and thankfully home.

At Colorado State, I always ended my Animal Breeding classes in the kilt with Burns poems in hand for the cowboys' edification, and I was, as well, invited year after year to talk to the literature classes when they came to the section on Romantic Poets, and I read Burns in genuine Scots. The students confessed that, though they had had an introduction to Burns in High School, they had never really appreciated him till I talked about his life and read his works. Thus it was that in the giving of Burns I loved and learned many of his more famous poems by heart.

In 1983, I went to Lebanon to be Dean of Agriculture at the American University of Beirut – in 1985 I was kidnapped by Islamic Jihad without my book of Burns.

During six-and-a-half years chained to the wall, when with fellow captives, I insisted every January 25 that we celebrate Burns – the Brits mostly bored, Terry Anderson mostly interested. Two anniversaries stand out more clearly than the others. January 25 of 1987, and I was in isolation, no one to talk to, no one to listen to Burns, so I celebrated on my own. I recited quietly as many of the poems as I could recall – 'To a Mouse', 'To a Louse', 'Holy Willie's Prayer', 'John Anderson My Jo', 'Flow Gently Sweet Afton' . . . and on and on . . . Two hundred and nine years were as nothing when I recited the poem that both Jean and I loved above all others, 'My Love is like a Red, Red Rose' and it brought her close. Several of his longer poems I had never totally memorized, so I struggled with these. But thankfully – for 'Tam o' Shanter' and 'The Cotter's Saturday Night' occupied many a lonely and tedious captivity hour in isolation, as I tried to get all the couplets in their correct order. He saved me that night.

The other Burns anniversary – January 25, 1988 – I was in the company of Jean-Paul Kauffman, who was also, like Terry, most interested in Burns, although he confessed to knowing almost nothing of him or his verse. It was an enormous challenge to translate Burns into French, but I did my best, and Jean-Paul was truly touched by the Bard. Some years later, after my release, Jean-Paul came over to Scotland,

and together we visited many of Burns' haunts all over Ayrshire, making the documentary film *Burns in Beirut*. And I'll never forget it – we visited the Cottage and saw Burns' birth bed, and Jean-Paul stood in awe and proclaimed, 'Ze bed of genius . . .'

Yes . . . it's been sixty years, but Burns touched me early and has had, and always will have, a very special place in my life.

But Mousie, thou art no thy lane,
In proving foresight may be vain:
The best-laid schemes o mice an men
Gang aft agley,
An lea'e us nought but grief an pain,
For promis'd joy!

To a Mouse. *On turning her up in her nest with the plough, November 1785*

Nicky Spence

Opera Singer

My passion for Burns has turned into an unadulterated love affair with age, but something has always been there, from the first time I heard about that 'wee, sleeket, cowran, tim'rous beastie' to every time I sing 'My luve is like a red red rose' today.

Burns writes beautifully for the voice, and although I'm an opera singer by training, I see Scottish song as of equal importance to all my repertoire, and as it's so fantastic to sing, I approach it the same way I would a Mozart aria.

Having grown up in Dumfries and having the pleasure of claiming Burns' burial ground as my regular place of worship, it's such a pleasure to collaborate with an artist whose passion, like my own, was nurtured in south west Scotland. I was very lucky to be able to put quite a few Burns tunes on my debut album *My First Love*, and I get really excited as Burns Night season approaches, not only as I get to consume enough haggis to sink a small Hebridean island, but I get to sing all these fantastic songs exclusively every night for two weeks.

'Ae Fond Kiss' is said to encapsulate the sentiments of a thousand love songs, and I think, as my favourite piece, it is a true example of Burns' honest and timeless writing, which has been a real inspiration in my own career.

> Had we never lov'd sae kindly,
> Had we never lov'd sae blindly!
> Never met – or never parted –
> We had ne'er been broken-hearted.

One thing's for sure, I'm a truly lucky lad to be from a land which allows me to sing Burns from the heart, and I know if he were around today, he'd certainly be laden with Grammys and other awards for his songwriting.

The Burns Mausoleum, St Michael's Kirkyard, Dumfries

In 1817, Burns' remains were moved here from their original resting place. Jean Armour, Robert's wife, is buried beside Burns in the Mausoleum.

Brian Cox

Actor

Robert Burns was the quintessential Scotsman – charming, rebellious, inspiring and inspired. His maverick spirit has been a vital source of inspiration to me – I love that he found artistic inspiration through the history and politics (not to mention the lovely women) of Scotland.

Our history is a rich one, and is where I find a lot of my own ambition and drive. And Burns' own legend is a great part of that. That he spoke to and for Scots, working-class Scots, not the nobility, is where I draw perhaps the greatest nostalgia for him.

The Americans may have Robert Frost, but we have Robert Burns, and I'll take his sensational bawdy lyrics, filled with such spirit and passion, over Frost's tame pastoral meditations any day.

There was a lad was born in Kyle,
But whatna day o whatna style,
I doubt it's hardly worth the while
  To be sae nice wi Robin.

Robin was a rovin boy,
  Rantin, rovin, rantin, rovin,
Robin was a rovin boy,
  Rantin, rovin Robin!

Rantin, Rovin Robin

Andrew O'Hagan

Writer, UNICEF Ambassador

Someone rang the other day to tell me that my old school was being demolished. I don't mind telling you I felt a stab of grief, not because I loved school so terribly much at the time I was there, but for a Scottish person, or perhaps any kind of person, a loss of the past can be experienced like a certain draining of the blood. Not far from that Ayrshire school, maybe two or three miles, there was a house we lived in long ago. Last time I went to Scotland I decided on a whim to go and look at the house. My parents were never very happy there, but I realized, as I drove through the countryside, that the place had lived very vividly in my dreams. In some senses, I had never stopped thinking about it, and as the car drew closer I began to feel nervous – I hadn't been there in 25 years.

It was an empty field. The house was gone, and so were all the surrounding buildings. They must have been taken down some time ago, because the grass was grown over and the natural world – always so present in my childhood, though pressed into the background by breeze-blocks and migrant human troubles and urban planning – had recovered its former position, wild bushes and cows predominant, and suddenly like eternal ghosts in that memorial Ayrshire landscape. I walked over the grass plucking berries, and I took a plump, early bramble from one of the bushes and deliberately ate it, feeling good, almost relieved, to be able to ingest something of this place on a cold day, something natural and sustaining. And in that moment I thought of Robert Burns, the passage in *Tam o' Shanter* about fading time:

> But pleasures are like poppies spread:
> You seize the flow'r, its bloom is shed;
> Or like the snow falls in the river,
> A moment white – then melts for ever;
> Or like the borealis race,
> That flit ere you can point their place;
> Or like the rainbow's lovely form
> Evanishing amid the storm.
> Nae man can tether time or tide,
> The hour approaches Tam maun ride.

The person who caused me to fall in love with the poems and songs of Robert Burns was my head-mistress, Mrs Ferguson. She played very nicely on an upright piano in the gym hall, and it was my job – being 10 or so, and hopelessly flamboyant – to sing beside her the song 'My Love She's But a Lassie Yet'. I can still see the flush of pleasure in her cheek as I sang the words with an accent full of local in-nocence. The other boys were out playing football and she behaved as if we were co-conspirators in a secret legion of art-lovers. From that day I have loved Robert Burns and all who sail in him, the words growing in my mind as I myself have grown away from that boy, feeling the lines only more keenly with the passing decades and the distance between that Ayrshire summer and me. It is Robert Burns who bridges the gap, and always will, creating a unity of selves and seasons, making a home for mice and men in the natural order.

But pleasures are like poppies spread:
You seize the flow'r, its bloom is shed;
Or like the snow falls in the river,
A moment white – then melts for ever…

Tam o' Shanter

Rory Macdonald

Musician. Founding member of Runrig

I spent most of my childhood on North Uist in the Western Isles, at a time during the fifties, before television and electricity had impacted upon island life. I was privileged to have caught the final years of the old, Gaelic way of life; one that was about to be altered irrevocably as the onward march of twentieth century technology made its mark.

During these early years, our entertainment was largely spontaneous and self-created, with friends and family always calling on one another. I can vividly recall the storytelling and singing that played such a part in our lives. One favoured family ritual was to gather round the wireless (its use had to be rationed, as the large battery that powered it was both expensive and limited in output) and listen in, on Friday and Saturday evenings, to Radio Luxembourg's Scottish and Irish request programmes – one of the few sources available to hear traditional music. Often, neighbours would come round, sharing the experience and joining in with the songs and music that became the soundtrack to my childhood years.

It was here that I first encountered Burns, initially in the more popular songs of the day sung by Scottish tenors like Robert Wilson or played within Scottish dance sets by accordion and fiddle bands like Jimmy Shand and Ian Powrie.

The great love songs like 'Ae Fond Kiss', 'Ye Banks and Braes', and 'My Love Is like a Red, Red Rose' were frequently broadcast, and although, as a Gaelic speaker, some of the Scots used in the lyrics might have seemed an alien tongue to me, nevertheless the feeling that came out of these songs was richly potent and made a lasting impression.

I took up my first instrument, the piano accordion, when I was about eight, and these melodies soon made their way on to the keys, my initial bad habit of only playing on the black notes finding a suitable companion in 'Ye Banks and Braes'!

The popularly held image of Burns is as a poet, first and foremost, with his melodies gleaned from various external sources: folk tunes, Gaelic melodies, bits of other popular melodies that he came across and adapted, and that these were secondary to his words, almost an afterthought. I'd say that it's not just his poetry but the combined effect of it with music that has helped create his magnificent body of work. It matters little that he may not have written completely original melodies. His genius was in the way he married his sources, the way the words and the music combined in that inextricable way that defines brilliant songwriting. I'm sure that Burns never considered his melodies as afterthoughts – but rather that they were crafted and felt in the same way as his words were.

His songs have remained, throughout my life, as inspiring and tangible a part of Scotland as the mountains and the lochs, permanently intertwined – like they've always been there.

His gift is that they will continue to inspire people all over the world until the very end of time.

Ye banks and braes o bonie Doon,
  How can ye bloom sae fresh and fair?
How can ye chant, ye little birds,
  And I sae weary fu o care!
Thou'll break my heart, thou warbling bird,
  That wantons thro the flowering thorn!
Thou minds me o departed joys,
  Departed never to return.

The Banks o Doon

Lord George Robertson
Former NATO Secretary General

For an admirer of the poetry and songs of Robert Burns there can be few more delicious experiences than to introduce him to the uninitiated. To open the eyes and ears of someone who is yet to experience the wonder and the majesty of Burns' work is a real pleasure.

We, in Scotland, perhaps take him and his magic too much for granted. We celebrate all through January – and, increasingly, much longer, and we indulge in a wealth of reading, singing and valuing the Bard. The love affair goes on and on. But in spite of his international appeal and the global reach of his message, much of the world has still to feel the power and the beauty of Scotland's peasant poet.

When I was Secretary General of NATO, and based in the European capital of Brussels, I found the ideal opportunity to do some Burns missionary work. The American Ambassador to NATO (now number three in the US State Department) was actually called Robert (Nick) Burns. His father had been a fan.

We hatched the idea of a first ever NATO Burns Supper with invitations to all the Ambassadors in NATO's forty-six nation Partnership for Peace. In aid of Scotland's veterans' home, Erskine Hospital, the evening would be a first for the world's most successful Defence Alliance.

But the joy of the occasion was not just in the music of Fiona Kennedy, the 'Lassies' Reply' from Helen Liddell to Ambassador Graham Hewitt, the well-appreciated Bowmore malt or butcher John Hill's magnificent haggis from Dunblane. It came in the dawning awareness among the Ambassadors of a cultural phenomenon. Here were words from two centuries ago speaking of today's feelings, and melodies protected from the past making beautiful music of today.

From Central Asia, from the Balkans, from Eastern Europe and from North America, people who had never heard of Robert Burns marvelled at a blend of words sparkling with contemporary relevance and vitality. Oh yes, it was a great evening for spreading the Rabbie message.

And another such evening also comes to mind. In Dumfries in 1996, there was a meeting of all Scotland's MPs. It was held in the town where Burns died and where his mausoleum dominates the local graveyard. We had assembled for a debate on Scotland's future with the intriguing import of Britain's then Prime Minister, John Major. It was a characteristic Scottish political occasion – noisy, rude, boisterous and not greatly productive, but nonetheless a bruising eye-opener for the visiting PM.

But that same evening saw an event which brought the warring parties together. The then Scottish Secretary, Michael Forsyth, had organised a Burns Supper to mark the 200th anniversary of the Bard's early death. In an inspired and generous thought he had asked a political opponent, Donald Dewar, to give the Immortal Memory.

I drove with Donald to the function and tried to help him unscramble a thousand pieces of seemingly random notes from his car boot. The venture seemed doomed. But Donald took the hotch potch of thoughts, notes and quotes, and armed with his transparently reverential views delivered a masterpiece

Immortal Memory to the assembled cocktail of political foes. Once again a great advocate had spread the message of Burns' lasting legacy.

It was a truly memorable, and significant, evening where Scotland's political elite (every party claiming Burns as their own) celebrated that brief, brilliant life of talent and wonder, which had come to an end two hundred years before in the town where we met.

Robert Burns' mortal remains lie in the modest mausoleum there in Dumfries, and when you visit it you cannot be unaffected. But his life's work lives on by illuminating lives down the ages and across the continents.

And every year, more and more people come to know and understand and enjoy the sheer magic of the Ayrshire poet who was to become Scotland's national bard.

Ellisland Farm, Dumfriesshire

The Spence Window, by which the poet completed Tam o' Shanter, having composed it while repeatedly walking between the farmhouse and the banks of the River Nith

Richard Demarco

Artist and Art Promoter

'The Birks of Aberfeldy' is the one poem by Robert Burns that has inspired me more than any other. It is not one of his most famous or, indeed, one of his best, and yet it has managed to give me the feeling of his physical presence to such an extent that, following in his Highland journeys, I can now see aspects of his beloved Scotland directly through his eyes.

Aberfeldy is at the heart of Highland Perthshire. It was unfamiliar territory for Burns, and part of the most northerly section of his 1787 tour of the Scottish Highlands which led him to the picturesque village of Kenmore, overlooking the eastern waters of Loch Tay, with a view towards the alpine grandeur of Ben More.

At the Kenmore Inn, he found comfort and rest and warmed himself before its main fireplace. Now, two hundred years later, on the whitewashed wall directly above the fireplace, protected by a sheet of glass, can be seen the words of 'Verses Written with a Pencil over the Chimney-piece in the Parlour of the Inn at Kenmore'.

What prompted him to write upon that rough surface? Was it an impulse? Was he urged to do so in conversation? Could he imagine his delicate pencil marks would endure into the twenty-first century as proof of his earthly presence?

Standing before that fireplace, comforted on a cold autumn afternoon by the heat of burning logs, it was not difficult for me to imagine Robert Burns occupying the exact same space, leaning against the wall to gain a point of balance in order to write the words of the poem.

'The Birks of Aberfeldy' had been composed whilst climbing the winding path that enabled him to negotiate the steeply rising, rock-strewn terrain of the tree-covered slopes of what, in certain places, is no more than a narrow ledge dramatically separating the two banks of the mountain stream known as the Urlar Burn as it makes its way from the spectacular Falls of Moness towards the River Tay, via the Aberfeldy Watermill.

The Mill is now transformed into a bookshop and art gallery, with most of its architectural features, both internal and external, lovingly restored by Kevin and Jayne Ramage. They invited me to exhibit paintings, drawings and prints, with a special focus on what I have defined as 'The Road to Meikle Seggie', my favourite archetypal Scottish drovers' road which wends its way through Perthshire, leading, eventually, to a fabled land which the Gaelic-speaking bardic poets recognised as 'Tír na nÓg', 'The Land of the Ever Young', when, on midsummer day, the light of the sunset and the sunrise are inseparable.

This autumn, I conducted two master-classes under the aegis of the Watermill Gallery, inspired by the unchanging reality of what Robert Burns defines in what is essentially a love poem.

> Now Simmer blinks on flow'ry braes,
> And o'er the crystal streamlets plays,
> Come, let us spend the lightsome days
> In the birks of Aberfeldy.

Such an Arcadian wonderland in all the seasons of the year makes Aberfeldy a nodal point on the Road to Meikle Seggie. It is a place to explore most carefully, with your every step taking you closer to a world forever blessed by a poet whose sublime gifts enabled him to personify the physical reality of Scotland and its unique splendour.

It is a place which invites you to delight in the relationship of the birch trees to the sound and sight of water cascading and tumbling through a mesmerising variety of rock pools, set in luxuriant undergrowth, and illuminated by the light of the sky filtered through multilayered canopies of trees.

Robert Burns knew that this is a place where local legend has declared that you can be sure to find a fairyland, where water spirits are in command, to reveal the sacred element beyond the stuff and substance of Nature. He knew that Highland Scotland abounds in such legends. Thank heavens that he saw it as his self-appointed task to write a poem in praise of an enduring legend and to make it manifest in an anthology of poetry.

Th' outstretching lake, imbosomed 'mong the hills,
The eye with wonder and amazement fills…

Verses Written with a Pencil over the Chimney-piece, in the Parlour of the Inn at Kenmore, Taymouth

John Lowrie Morrison (Jolomo)

Artist

Robert Burns is my favourite poet and always has been… Oh, I've drifted away from time to time to the New England poets like Walt Whitman and Robert Frost… and when at Glasgow School of Art professed allegiance to surreal or existential poets… meeting in various poetry groups where we would do our D.P.S. stuff, reading aloud, probably the weirdest poems we could find just to sound cool!

However, I always secretly loved the work of Burns and loved it with all my heart – for Burns had 'touched' me as a child. In the mid 1950s at Dowanhill Primary School in Glasgow's west end, Burns was taught avidly from an early age. Every child had to be able to recite Burns without a mistake! Aged 6, I could recite and sing 'Wee Willie Gray's Wallet.' At age 8, I could recite 'To a Mouse' and 'To the Owl'. And at the age of 10, reciting *Tam o' Shanter* held no terrors for me – except that of standing up in front of a class of 53 to recite the poem.

Although we had to learn Burns… I loved his work… it evoked a magical and mysterious world which coloured my view of Scotland.

Although Burns is probably most famous for his love poems – 'Ae Fond Kiss' being, for me, the greatest love poem of all time – the work that inspires me most are the poems that are evocative of the Scottish landscape, weather and seasons. These resonate with my painting and my vision of Scotland. I still read Robert Burns often.

On a quiet moment in the studio… in between painting… I will read his works with inspiration… as I carry a tartan-bound miniature collection of his poems and songs in my studio jacket pocket – like another hero of mine, Abraham Lincoln, who also carried a small Burns collection in his jacket pocket and was also 'Touched by Burns'. Maybe Burns inspired Lincoln along the road of equality for all… he certainly inspired and still inspires me to paint the Scottish landscape!

Loud blaw the frosty breezes,
  The snaws the mountains cover.
Like winter on me seizes,
  Since my young Highland rover
  Far wanders nations over.

The Young Highland Rover

Rt. Hon. Charles Kennedy

Former Leader of Liberal Democrats

Being born and bred in the West Highlands, there was always, growing up as a youngster, a certain feeling that Burns didn't touch us in quite the same way as elsewhere in Scotland. Certainly, there were the obligatory annual suppers, and the melodies and songs always featured in local ceilidhs; it was just that we were more influenced by being part of Gaeldom.

Over the decades there is no doubt that the steady influx of southern Scots into the area has moved us in a more Burns-orientated direction. Yet, the irony here is that Burns himself had rather pronounced views about the Highlands, as he remarked upon visiting the Duke of Argyll at Inveraray in June 1787. When he arrived the Duke was having a large house party. The landlord was too busy attending to the Duke's guests to have time for passing travellers. Burns responded:

> There's naething here but Highland pride,
>   And Highland scab and hunger;
> If Providence has sent me here
>   'Twas surely in an anger.

In subsequent centuries, mercifully, the Highland condition has been transformed for the better; meanwhile the universal appeal of Burns continues undiminished. And, of course, it is that very universality which enables practising politicians the world over to extract a particular quotation – often out of context – to help imply that if Burns was with us today he would in all likelihood be 'one of us' party politically. Best to add a pinch of salt to your haggis and neeps next time you hear a politician proposing 'The Immortal Memory'.

He does send such politically mixed messages that it is little wonder he can be open to widely varying interpretations. On one level, we're all liable to be dismissed as no more than 'a parcel of rogues', yet throughout his work runs a passionate concern about the lot of his fellow man.

For myself, I have always considered Burns – given his interest in ideas as well as his impatience over social progress – in fact to be more understanding of the necessity for politics and public representation, whatever the constraints involved. A thinker and a doer are led inexorably towards public policy enactment – i.e. politics. I think Burns understood that only too well, even if he was your quintessential example of today's floating voter. He would, in our contemporary technological age, be a supreme polemicist on his Burns blog; pity someone trying to be his local MP!

So, leaving aside party political praying-in-aid, the best way in which ALL politicians should be touched by Burns is to look in the mirror regularly and think, not vanity, but instead check yourself constantly against the charge of hypocrisy. Hold consistent ideals, fairly applied, with a constant focus on the social realities round about you. If you stick to that approach, it seems to me, then you are more likely to navigate the occasionally treacherous waters which can surround you.

There is also an alternative parliamentary Selkirk Grace, always worth recalling:

> Some hae seats they cannae keep
> And some nae seat but want it;
> But we wi' seats that we did keep
> For that the Lord be thankit.

Amen to that; if you can recite it then you have indeed been touched by Burns.

Farewell to the mountains, high-cover'd with snow,
Farewell to the straths and green valleys below,
Farewell to the forests and wild-hanging woods,
Farewell to the torrents and loud-pouring floods!

My Heart's in the Highlands

Andy Hall
Photographer

'A rich and cultivated, but still unenclosed country' is how Robert Burns described the Mearns in Kincardineshire in the north east of Scotland, the land of his forefathers, when he visited the area in 1787.

I have lived in Stonehaven for most of my life, and I often drive and walk through the landscape that Burns' ancestors, from his father back to his great-great-grandfather, knew so intimately. The family roots of Robert Burns are firmly embedded in the Mearns. This is the land of his fathers, the cradle of his family.

The Burnes (original spelling) family had worked the farms of Bogjurgen and Brawlinmuir before Robert's grandfather (also Robert) settled at Clochnahill, six miles south-west of Stonehaven, in the estate of Dunnottar. He had four sons, George (who died very young), James, Robert, and William, the poet's father.

As young men, William and his elder brother Robert left the Mearns together, driven southward by poor farming opportunities, a sense of adventure and the hope of better fortune. They parted, most probably, on the summit of the Garvock Hill near Laurencekirk, William going to Edinburgh and his brother Robert on to England, returning later to Dreghorn in Ayrshire.

When I stand above the Howe of the Mearns on the Garvock Hill, I can imagine the brothers leaving each other and William turning to take a last look towards the land of his birth and his brother, never to see them again. In later years, when the poet's father described this parting to his children, the word that he used to describe the intensity of his feelings was 'anguished'.

William reached Edinburgh to find work as a gardener, saving and sending money home to his elderly father. From Edinburgh, he found his way to Alloway in Ayrshire, where, after his marriage to Agnes Brown, the infant Robert was born.

I cannot find myself at the Garvock viewpoint without thinking of the brothers and their roads dividing for the last time. My favourite Burns poem, 'Ae Fond Kiss', is the most evocative description of parting that I have ever read.

'Ae farewell, alas, for ever!'

I like to think that the seeds of parting that touched the poet so deeply, and allowed him to find the beautifully perfect words for the poem, were sown on Garvock Tap that afternoon.

From time to time, I sit among the ruins of Brawliemuir (derived from Brawlinmuir) where the poet's grandfather, also Robert, was born, and think of the unforgiving and unyielding earth around me that was to be found again in Ayrshire by young Robert. The arduous existence endured by the poet in his early farming days was to be a significant contributory factor to the weakening of his heart and, ultimately, the shortening of his life.

One of life's pleasures for me is to immerse myself in the light and landscape of the Mearns with my camera, early in the morning or in the late afternoon, capturing the characteristic clear, soft, golden light with lengthening shadows modelling the undulating surface and contours of the land.

I often reflect that this is the same landscape that had, through previous generations, helped to mould and shape the character and philosophy of Robert Burns.

Ae fond kiss, and then we sever!
Ae farewell, and then forever!
Deep in heart-wrung tears I'll pledge thee,
Warring sighs and groans I'll wage thee.

Ae Fond Kiss

Sir Tom Hunter

Businessman and Philanthropist

What can you say about an Ayrshire man who even had Abe Lincoln stumped? When asked about the Bard, Lincoln is said to have responded: 'I cannot frame a toast to Burns. I can say nothing worthy of his generous heart, and transcendent genius.'

Burns to me sums us Scots up in the main – witty, generous, often incisive and only occasionally drunk! Like Carnegie, he is another Scot who has left an indelible mark on the world, a mark to make all us Scots proud... My close friend Rab Wilson, poet, takes much of his inspiration from Burns, as do I and many other Scots, and he constantly reminds me of our crucial role in delivering the Enlightenment to the world.

As Scots, we should be very proud of our heritage, but also remind ourselves that we too are creating the heritage today for future generations to enjoy – let's hope we make them equally proud, after all 'Wha's like us?'

How lofty, sweet Afton, thy neighbouring hills,
Far mark'd with the courses of clear, winding rills!
There daily I wander, as noon rises high,
My flocks and my Mary's sweet cot in my eye.

Sweet Afton

Dougie Donnelly

BBC Sports Presenter

In an age when the term 'genius' is almost as overused as 'celebrity', it is reassuring to remember a Scot who was thoroughly deserving of the description. I have loved Burns' work since my schooldays, and have always been impressed by the fact that his genius took so many forms. He was a poet, of course, but also an inspired songwriter and satirist.

I am always intrigued by what drives successful individuals, and Burns' humble background gives us few hints of the literary giant and great humanitarian that he would become, other than the fact that he was greatly influenced by his father William, a man of high ideals and principles. Who could fail to be inspired by such an example?

But there are other aspects of Burns' character that appeal to me greatly. He was an outspoken critic of the establishment of the day, and, even more important, very much one of the lads! He was a wit and raconteur and obviously a man who enjoyed a good night out. I think I would have relished bumping into Burns and Souter Johnny, his 'ancient, trusty, drouthy crony'!

Picture those 'reaming swats, that drank divinely' as the 'night drave on wi' sangs and clatter'. I have always felt there was a lot of the Bard in poor, terrified Tam o' Shanter! Not a po-faced bore, full of his own importance, but a 24-carat genius who also knew how to enjoy himself – Burns would have done for me!

On a much more prosaic level, my life would surely have turned out very differently had it not been for Rabbie, for it was while I was toasting the Lassies at a Burns Supper thirty years ago that a BBC producer suggested that I might have a future as a TV broadcaster!

We are na fou, we're nae that fou,
  But just a drappie in our e'e!
The cock may craw, the day may daw,
  And ay we'll taste the barley bree!

Willie Brew'd a Peck o Maut

Lord MacFarlane of Bearsden

Chairman of the Kelvingrove Refurbishment Appeal

When asked what Robert Burns has meant to me throughout my life, I discovered how difficult a question that was. Burns means so many different things to so many different people, including me, but it didn't take me long to recognise that Burns was a man who couldn't abide hypocrisy. Perhaps too often for his own sake, he spoke the truth regardless.

I sympathise with his dislike of wars, as shown so well in these lines from his poem, 'The Tree of Liberty':

> Wi plenty o sic trees, I trow,
> > The warld would live in peace, man;
> The sword would help to mak a plough,
> > The din o war wad cease, man.

How pertinent for our world today! So this philosophy, and the others he propounded throughout his woefully short life, have inspired me over the years.

His religion: 'I am drawn to the Bible by the conviction of a man, and not by a halter.'

His distaste of human pride:

> O wad some Power the giftie gie us
> To see oursels as ithers see us!
> It wad frae monie a blunder free us,
> > An foolish notion.

His wish: 'If I had one wish, it would be to wipe away all tears from all eyes.'

Robert Burns had a unique ability to write of simple things, like the fate of the wounded hare, or the loss of the mountain daisy that he turned down with the plough; probably the same plough which destroyed the nest of the little field mouse. In so doing, he embraced all mankind by comparing their fate to his.

I have had a lifelong interest in the visual arts, so I was delighted to find in Burns one of the greatest landscape painters of all time. His pictures were, of course, in words, but are every bit as vivid as the greatest examples of Turner or Constable. When he writes of his beloved woodlands, streams and flora, these become living pictures in our minds.

For a' that, an' a' that, he has had an immense influence on me throughout my life, but if I had to sum up in just a few words what I believe to be his greatest gift to humanity, then it would be his heartfelt plea that one day there might be a brotherhood of man.

Then let us pray that come it may,
    As come it will for a' that,
That Sense and Worth o'er a' the earth,
    Shall bear the gree, and a' that.
For a' that, an a' that,
    It's comin yet for a' that,
That Man to Man the world o'er
    Shall brithers be for a' that.

Among the heathy hills and ragged woods
The roaring Fyers pours his mossy floods;
Till full he dashes on the rocky mounds,
Where, thro a shapeless breach, his stream resounds.

Lines on the Falls of Fyers, near Loch Ness

Gavin Esler

Broadcaster, Writer and Journalist

I cannot remember a time BB – Before Burns. My Uncle Jim, who lived near Aberfeldy with a stretch of the Tay for a front garden, recited *Tam o' Shanter* to me as a child, and told me tales (suitably censored) of the Bard's life and exploits.

'The only concomitant with Burns,' Uncle Jim would say, reaching for the malt, 'is a good whisky.'

From school in Edinburgh, I would walk through the Grassmarket to get my bus home, aware, somehow, that the Scottish capital is a Dr Jekyll and Mr Hyde city, just like Burns himself. The Bard was simultaneously a Romantic rapscallion and a dull exciseman. Perhaps this is why Burns touches me so deeply; he is at the heart of our strange Scottish split personality.

We are a calculating culture of accountants, scientists and engineers, and a mad, passionate culture of patriotism, anger and Celtic darkness. I would pass the monuments to both posh old Walter Scott and the living Grassmarket roughnecks who were much more the Burns milieu. For a teenager, there was no contest. Everything about Burns is what gangsta rappers would call ba-aaaaad – bad, as in instantly attractive, on the edge of law-abiding, decent society.

As a teenager I read Burns' life and his poems, read how he loved with passion and with loss – 'Ae Fond Kiss', the anthem of teenage love-lorn angst. I read how he loathed the Holy Willies around us – 'Holy Willie's Prayer', the anthem of teenage rebellion against the hypocrites who rule our lives.

'Oh, Lord – yestreen – thou kens – wi' Meg…'

Oh, yes, we all kent about Holy Willie. I had one as a neighbour. Two, actually. And then there is the wonderful ability of Burns to elude us all, refusing to be stuffed into convenient political boxes. I remember a particularly nationalist friend who kept wittering about Burns and the 'language' of Lallans. Unfortunately Burns himself sub-titles his first volume of poems *Chiefly in the Scottish Dialect* (1786). He knew the difference.

Then there were my hairy leftie friends who held up Burns as a Communist prototype. Unfortunately for them, the poet makes clear that a man's a man for a' that — a man is not just a unit of Stalinist production. Burns' ethics were not from communism but from humanity.

In recent years, I've travelled everywhere from the Aleutian Islands to Iran, from China to Peru, and back again. In the strangest places I've had cause to remember Burns and to quote him – sometimes with a bit of explanation for the locals.

Whether it is George Bush in front of a sign saying 'Mission Accomplished' or Mahmoud Ahmedinejad speechifying in Tehran, some Israeli politician, or a Kremlin apparatchik, or even, God forbid, some of us self-important folk on television, Burns has the ultimate insight:

O wad some Power the giftie gie us
To see oursels as ithers see us!
It wad frae monie a blunder free us,
An foolish notion.

O wad some Power the giftie gie us
To see oursels as ithers see us!
It wad frae monie a blunder free us,
An foolish notion:
What airs in dress an gait wad lea'e us,
An ev'n devotion!

To a Louse. *On Seeing One on a Lady's Bonnet at Church*

Sir Malcolm Rifkind

Former Foreign Secretary and Secretary of State for Scotland

Robert Burns is an extraordinary phenomenon. I say 'is', not 'was'. Every year, Scots, both at home and abroad, remember him with Burns Suppers, and have done so since he died around 200 years ago. Why? The English don't have annual Shakespeare Dinners. The Russians don't have Tolstoy Lunches. And the French, so far as I am aware, don't have Voltaire Breakfasts.

What's so special about Burns? Perhaps the answer can be found in the fact that he is remembered by Suppers, by nature a modest and rather informal meal.

Burns was a people's poet, both with the material he used and the audience to whom his poems were addressed. He rescued many of the traditional songs and rhymes of rural Scotland from oblivion just in the nick of time.

So I enjoy either reading Burns or hearing him being recited because it happens naturally, with neither a great mental effort being required nor with the feeling that one has moved from the ordinary world into some intellectual salon.

But I am also touched by Burns because he remains so highly relevant to the threats, problems and opportunities of modern life, including those of the political world.

We live, we are told, in an age of spin when wicked governments and politicians try to hide their misdeeds and exaggerate their achievements in order to retain their power and their privileges. Burns understood this very well. Remember these splendid lines:

> Here's freedom to him that wad read,
> Here's freedom to him that wad write!
> There's nane ever fear'd that the Truth should be heard,
> But they whom the truth would indite.'

So Burns championed freedom of speech. He punctured the pompous. He reminded the mighty that they had feet of clay like almost everyone else. And he tore away the veil of hypocrisy from both self-satisfied clergymen and sycophantic fellow travellers with such gentle but penetrating humour that his words still resonate today.

Of course he touches us still. I wouldn't be writing this article about him if he didn't!

The Meadows, Edinburgh

where William Burnes, the poet's father, found work as a gardener for two years after leaving the Mearns.
He then continued to Ayrshire, where he met Agnes Brown of Kirkoswald. They married in 1757.

Lord David Steel

Former Presiding Officer of the Scottish Parliament

The poetry of Robert Burns was, in my day, rather badly taught in school – with emphasis on trying to translate such lines as 'a daimen-icker in a thrave/'S a sma' request'. It was only in later years, when as MP in the Scottish Borders I had to attend dozens of Burns Suppers – both authentic ones run by Burns Clubs, and genial amateur ones such as the Galashiels Cycling Club, which was held in a crowded remote pub in the Yarrow Valley on a cold windy night. The chairman on that occasion enlivened the proceedings by enquiring after every person returned from the loo: 'O were't thou in the cauld blast?'

These occasions, with a high standard of oratory extolling the life of Burns, beautiful singing and powerful recitation, changed my perspective on his work, and led me, in turn, to speak not only in Scotland but in Canada, New York, Nairobi, Portugal and Hungary, amongst others, on the life and work of the Bard.

My own favourite recitation (only for private events at Aikwood Tower complete with nightgown and candle) is the perceptive satire *Holy Willie's Prayer*. Politically there is nothing to beat 'A Man's a Man', which is why we had it at the reopening of the Scottish Parliament after 300 years' absence in 1999.

But, Lord, remember me and mine
Wi mercies temporal and divine,
That I for grace an gear may shine,
Excell'd by nane,
And a' the glory shall be Thine –
Amen, Amen!

Holy Willie's Prayer

Chris Dunlop

Mountaineer

In the closing months of 2005, over a pint or two, David Kerr, an old friend and debating partner from University, and myself got together and came up with the idea of holding the world's highest ever Burns Supper on Aconcagua, the highest mountain in the world outside of the Himalayas, on Burns' birthday, 25th January 2006. David had been there at the start of my Burns experience, when I organised my first Burns Supper in 1990 while an undergraduate student at St Andrews University. When I'm coming up with project ideas, David is my sounding board.

A company in Ayrshire made up a special 'Burns Supper in a Tin' of haggis, neeps and tatties, and off to Argentina I went. The landscape couldn't have contrasted more with that of Scotland in January. It was blisteringly hot, to the point where your skin would burn beneath your clothing, the landscape was cruel and arid, and you couldn't get a decent pint of beer anywhere!

However, the spirit of adventure, passion and pride drove me on. Further up, the beauty and awe of the mountain came into view: snow-capped peaks, thrusting glacial rivers, the majestic condors flying high above. We reached base camp and rested in preparation for our assault on the mountain. After acclimatisation, the final assault began.

The groundwork was set, the route was planned and the resources put into place. However, as with all these things, 'the best-laid schemes o' mice an' men gang aft agley'. The expedition guide fell ill, the back-up guide didn't turn up and team members were suffering from the effects of altitude and exhaustion.

We ploughed on, however, and three days later we were at the advanced camp, ready for a day of rest, and the final and ultimate point, the summit. However, our best-laid plans were once again put on hold; injuries had been acquired, and more importantly, the hand dealt to us by God changed. We went from a straight flush to a pair of jokers, the weather turned.

We sat it out, but our measurements were that the weather was deteriorating, and rapidly. We began to descend from 21,000 feet. However, the effects of exhaustion and altitude severely affected members. An English colleague fell. I went to his rescue and got him off the mountain but in the process, slipped on ice, broke three ribs and damaged my knee. In various states of disrepair and exhaustion, we made a tactical retreat.

The Burns Supper, or Breakfast as it was, took place at 6am the following morning. The tin of haggis wasn't quite opened in the traditional way; the first time, surely, of the haggis being liberated from its encasement by ice axe. I made the Address to the Haggis, and various individuals from Norway, Finland, Spain and Argentina were co-opted to make the necessary speeches. The 'Toast to the Lassies' (or lack of!) was made, and a spirited response in Spanish came forth.

I phoned into the Scottish Parliament via satellite phone and, with an array of fractures and suffering from exposure and hypothermia, I belted out a verse of 'Auld Lang Syne' to an invited audience that had donated money to a nominated charity.

The Burns Supper was possibly the soberest I've ever been to. If Burns had wanted to change anything about our tribute to him, it would surely have been the prevalence of a greater flow of wine, women and song. Two days later, we arrived back in the 45 degrees heat of Mendoza and tried to play catch-up. Valiantly, we managed, but only on the wine and song. What we missed out on in terms of being 'Besides a sweet lassie, my thought and my dream', we more than compensated for on the other fronts.

It was the grandest of times, in memory of our grandest of poets; I hope a fitting tribute, and one he would have revelled in!

Ye Pow'rs, wha mak mankind your care,
And dish them out their bill o fare,
Auld Scotland wants nae skinking ware
            That jaups in luggies;
But, if ye wish her gratefu prayer,
            Gie her a Haggis!

Address to a Haggis

Sheena Wellington

Traditional Singer

The songs and poetry of Robert Burns have been part of my life forever. I grew up in a singing home with a grandmother who did the washing up while singing 'The De'il's awa wi' the Exciseman', and made the soup to the tune of 'Ae Fond Kiss'. My father was in high demand to sing at Burns Suppers, smokers and private dinners, and could recite *Tam o' Shanter* or *The Cottar's Saturday Night* on demand.

The name and, to some extent, the fame of Robert Burns seeped into my heart unnoticed, but it was when I read James Barke's fictionalised biography *The Immortal Memory* that what was to be a lifetime love affair really started.

I was lucky enough to be in my early teens when the bicentenary of Robert Burns' birth was celebrated, and I revelled in the school concerts, the special radio programmes and the newspaper and magazine articles.

It was then, too, that I made my official Burns Supper debut. As the event was all stag, I was only allowed in to sing, then spent my time in the kitchen with the women who were kindness itself and who fed me royally. The Supper itself was a lively affair and it was an eye-opener to see local dignitaries making total fools of themselves in drink!

But Robert's poetry and Robert's songs have been with me every day. I don't think I have ever got through 24 hours without singing at least a snatch of 'My Luve's like a Red, Red Rose', 'Ye Banks and Braes' or 'The Winter It Is Past', or without quoting Rab – 'The best laid schemes…' passes my lips quite often!

Apart from the beauty and the cleverness of his words and the wonderful tunes he set them to, it is Robert's palpable humanity that draws me. From his 'Address of Beelzebub' through 'Crookieden' and 'A Man's a Man for A' That' to 'A Poet's Welcome to his Love-Begotten Daughter', there breathes that warmth, that concern, that anger at cruelty, that rapscallion sense of humour that makes the fallible man and awe-inspiring genius that is Robert Burns. I love him – it's as simple as that.

Ae night the storm the steeples rocked;
Poor Labour sweet in sleep was locked;
While burns, wi snawy wreaths up-choked,
Wild-eddying swirl;
Or thro the mining outlet bocked,
Down headlong hurl.

A Winter Night

Joe Campbell

Honorary President of the Robert Burns World Federation

When I was very young I was, so I have been told, able to identify 78-rpm gramophone records by the colours of their labels. Many of these recordings were of the songs of Robert Burns and my early introduction to these led to a love of his songs and eventually to an interest in all his and other poetry.

My singing teacher, Marie Thomson (Mrs John Tainsh), taught me Burns songs, never failing to remind me that these required as much care as those of Beethoven and Schubert. She made me recognise that Burns had an acute sense of rhythm as well as being scrupulous in avoiding a harsh consonant or syllable in his love songs. These songs, 'My Luve is like a red, red rose', 'Afton Water', 'Mary Morison', 'Ae Fond Kiss' ('the essence of a thousand love tales', according to Sir Walter Scott), 'Ca the Yowes', 'A Rosebud by my Early Walk', 'Ye Banks and Braes' and so on, three hundred of them in all, are unsurpassed in any language for their tenderness. Only a man who understood and loved the lassies could ever pour such emotion into a few lines with such passion.

> Had we never lov'd sae kindly,
> Had we never lov'd sae blindly,
> Never met – or never parted –
> We had ne'er been broken-hearted.
> ('Ae Fond Kiss')

> Till a' the seas gang dry, my dear,
>   And the rocks melt wi the sun!
> And I will luve thee still, my dear,
>   While the sands o life shall run.
> ('My Luve Is Like a Red, Red Rose')

> O, Mary, can'st thou wreck his peace,
>   Wha for thy sake wad gladly die?
> Or canst thou break that heart of his,
>   Whase only faut is loving thee?
> ('Mary Morison')

How right Abraham Lincoln was when he said 'Robert Burns never touched a sentiment without carrying it to its ultimate expression, and leaving nothing further to be said.'

The four hundred or so poems written by Robert Burns were, almost without exception, inspired by nature in all her moods. By virtue of his genius he expanded them to embrace all of mankind. Who can resist the tale he tells of the wee field mouse whose nest he had inadvertently destroyed in the depth of winter, and whose cruel fate resembled that of others as well as himself?

Next year the world will remember the special birthday of the baby born on 25th January, 1759, who had little comfort or stability in his life other than his God-given genius. He was born in a blustery

January when the weather was as tempestuous and as unpredictable as his short life itself, a life in which he never flinched from telling the truth, even when it hurt him to do so. And yet, despite his hardship, or maybe even because of it, he rose above all worldly cares to become immortal, thereby justifying the common held belief that he was the greatest Scot who ever lived. His poems and songs are as relevant now as they were then, and how I agree with Hugh MacDiarmid's assertion:

'Rabbie, wad'st thou wert here – the warld hath need,
And Scotland mair sae, o' the likes o' thee!'

He was a gash an faithfu tyke,
As ever lap a sheugh or dyke.
His honest, sonsie, baws'nt face
Ay got him friends in ilka place.

The Twa Dogs

Catherine Lockerbie

Director of the Edinburgh International Book Festival

Burns is so deeply embedded in the bloodstream, it is sometimes hard to analyse when he first infiltrated my life. It is as if he has always been there, in the very air. Yet he was curiously absent from my Scottish state schooling. We did certainly sing his songs in the kind of innocent music class which now scarcely exists – a rag-tag bunch of ten-year-olds in ties and untucked shirts belting out 'Charlie Is My Darling' or 'Johnnie Cope'. We absorbed the tunes, a little history into the bargain, though very little formal sense of the prodigious, sprawling genius of the ploughman poet. Indeed for years, I thought these songs in some almost intrinsic way the melodies of my land, blithely unaware that Robert Burns had written or collected them. He was simply a name hanging around in the cultural hinterland, like Shakespeare. The shock of personal recognition, the plummeting into a love affair – that came later.

At every turn, though, there he was, throughout my childhood. Growing up in Bridge of Allan in the late sixties, I would spend entire days roaming the woods and hills on my own – a solitary nine-year-old tomboy with a head full of words. I loved the woods behind my house, through which I would scramble out onto the hills above. I loved the river and the peaty burn which flowed into it through a steep glen, the rich green crowding of the trees.

The song which I sang to myself on my stravaigings was 'The Lea-Rig'. I was not, in truth, sure what a lea-rig was – but I did know that the landscapes through which I ran were those of the poem, that I was seeing and feeling them through that prism – 'Down by the burn where scented birks/ Wi' dew are hanging clear, my jo' – and that beautiful image of the cattle heading home – 'And owsen frae the furrowed field/Return sae dowf and weary O.' I didn't know what 'dowf' meant either – I didn't need to, for as with much of Burns' Scots language, the meaning is right there in the very sound, in the way the word is cradled in the line.

And so, almost without realising it, I infused and fused my sensibilities with his. If, on the news, there was talk of nuclear Armageddon, if in the playground we terrified each other with tales of comets crashing into the earth. I knew about that, had felt it – 'Till a' the seas gang dry, my dear/ And the rocks melt wi' the sun.' A little older, I realised that 'A Red, Red Rose' is perhaps the most perfect love song ever. I had never felt that extraordinary, eternity-reaching love for anyone. In a sense I did not need to – I had the poem itself instead.

Later still, I actually learned about him, read more widely, encountered his impossible sexiness. His radicalism became part of the narrative of my life. The values of 'A Man's a Man for A' That', social justice and true democracy, are deep within me too. Aching love songs for the heart; political passion for the head; my soul seduced.

O, my luve is like a red, red rose,
That's newly sprung in June,
O, my luve is like the melodie,
That's sweetly play'd in tune.

My Luve Is Like a Red, Red Rose

Sally Magnusson

Television Presenter, Writer

Burns' poetry is all mixed up for me with memories of my mother. She is the one I rushed to, many years ago, when in a reckless moment I had agreed to do my first reply to the Toast to the Lassies. I phoned her up in a panic. This was a prestigious event, I squeaked. These people, I practically sobbed, would know their stuff. There would be hundreds of them. I had barely given Scotland's national bard a thought since learning 'To a Mouse' at primary school. I had never even been to a Burns Supper. What was I going to do?

My mother didn't hesitate. No greater love hath a woman than that she lay down her carefully crafted Burns speech for a daughter. 'Have mine,' she said.

The Burns Supper 'reply', which she breezily delivered down the phone that evening, was a revelation. Winding in and out of wry observations of Glasgow life from her time as a pioneering woman reporter on the Scottish Daily Express, and interspersed with well-aimed barbs at the men as required by the convention, there emerged an astute comment on the Burns Supper itself and the role that Robert Burns played in the 'poor benighted psyche of the Scottish male'. Why did Scottish men so hero-worship the Bard that they devoted a whole evening to celebrating his memory and singing the praises of the lassies in his name? Because, she argued, inarticulate as they famously are at expressing their deepest emotions, they find in Burns a champion who can do it for them.

Was she right? I bought myself a complete works, and for the first time in my life immersed myself in his poetry. I found there poems of such narrative power, such artful simplicity, such exhilarating range, that I couldn't believe I had reached so far into my twenties and successfully completed a degree in English Literature without discovering them.

And yet my mother was only half right. When it comes to the really deep and precious things of the heart and spirit, we all need Robert Burns to say it for us – not just the men. Which is why four lines of thirty words, each word consisting of only one unpretentious syllable, remain scratched right across my own heart.

They remind me of my mother and her merry laugh that day as she pointed me towards 'My Luve's like a red, red rose', the poem that opened my way to the rest of Burns' work. But they mean more than that, too. Shorn of their romantic context, and standing alone as simply the most perfect expression in the English language of yearning love, they express what I will always feel about her:

> Till a' the seas gang dry, my dear,
>   And the rocks melt wi' the sun:
> I will love thee still, my dear,
>   While the sands o' life shall run.

Till a' the seas gang dry, my dear,
And the rocks melt wi' the sun:
I will love thee still, my dear,
While the sands o' life shall run.

My Luve Is Like a Red, Red Rose

Jean Redpath

Traditional Singer

It was one of those unexpected, memorable moments that I fear will never be repeated. The westbound plane was half-empty, which is rare these days, and there was no movie on offer. Instead the woman ahead of me was actually talking with the American naval officer on his way home from the Holy Loch base.

I was buried in my book, until familiar lines caught my attention and I realised they were trading couplets from *Tam o' Shanter*. Quote for quote they stretched and strived until there was a pause, and a searching. No self-respecting performer could be expected to tolerate dead air, so I obliged with the next few lines. As I finished, a man walking up the aisle picked up the thread and continued the quote as he passed us. Everyone laughed and, I am sure, remembered that communion.

Another unforgettable moment that I hope will *not* be repeated: at the end of a performance I was taken somewhat by surprise when the host asked if I would lead the assembled company in 'Auld Lang Syne'. I was working with Serge Hovey at that point, so the tune that came out of my mouth was the one that Serge believed to be the version Burns intended for his song. It is close enough to the familiar one to make joining in very confusing for an audience, and after a verse and chorus, one man had had enough, and shouldered me off the microphone with the verdict 'That's the wrang tune!' I might take issue with his flagrant flouting of performance protocol, but I did admire his conviction, his passion, and his defence of the Bard (as he saw it!).

We look backward and see well over two hundred years of celebrations in the name of Burns, albeit mostly confined to two weeks of the year; to a comfortable familiarity with at least some of his work; to generations of education that encouraged rote memorization so that many of those same works lived on in the oral tradition, whence they came in the first place; to live performance where poems, and songs in particular, flourished away from the printed page.

I look forward and though I canna see, I guess (and fear) that technology and passivity will achieve, in a perilously short time, the death of what the indifference and neglect of the last two centuries have merely spared. What a richness of language has been lost to everyday usage since Burns mined it to such effect! Will there still *be* singers in fifty years?

But then again, Fergusson was already waxing elegiac about the death of music while Burns was still collecting it. Perhaps, like the hoodies, I am croaking for doom? I hope so… We may be taken over irrevocably by the iPods and the DVDs, the ear-buds and the MP3s, but:

> E'en then, a wish (I mind its pow'r),
> A wish that to my latest hour
>   Shall strongly heave my breast,
> That I for poor auld Scotland's sake
> Some usefu plan, or book could make,
>   Or sing a sang at least.
> *To the Guidwife of Wauchope House, Mrs Scott*

How lovely, Nith, thy fruitful vales,
Where bounding hawthorns gayly bloom,
And sweetly spread thy sloping dales,
Where lambkins wanton thro the broom!

The Banks of Nith

Bill Paterson

Actor

For most of us brought up in Scotland in the fifties, Robert Burns was the soundtrack of our school life. At primary school we recited his poems in that funny sing-song way and we belted out his songs in the school hall.

Some, like 'A Man's a Man', we loved right away. Others grew on us, but one teacher's obsession with 'Duncan Gray' had us hiding under our desks to avoid singing 'Ha, ha, the wooing o't'. That was a line we never really understood.

There was hardly a day when Burns wasn't with us. Then came the change. Throughout the sixties and seventies, Burns, the man of the people, the egalitarian republican with his sympathies for the French Revolution, seemed to be championed by some of the most conservative and narrow sections of Scottish life. We felt that, despite their love of his work, the last person they would have been at ease with would have been the complex and contradictory man himself.

Only John Cairney's passionate, charismatic portrayal of the bard, which came close to reincarnation, kept the flame alive for a lot of us. Time moved on, we grew up, and my generation came to realise how much we owed to Burns, not only for his own words but for his tireless collecting of our heritage. Truly a great man had lived in eighteenth century Scotland and today, singers like Dick Gaughan and Eddi Reader have helped bring him back to the very centre of our stage.

I've read his poems at the funerals of friends, I've addressed my fair share of Haggis and I've recorded the occasional CD. I've even made a misguided attempt to play the man on very late night television. The critic's words are still burned into my psyche. I was, he said, 'As feckless as a wither'd rash'. He was right.

Now we see in Burns all the contradictions and conflict of being Scots. The mist-shrouded romance of the Jacobite adventure and the clear new thinking of the enlightenment that would change Scotland and the world forever. The hard thankless labour in a beautiful but harsh landscape, and the late night carousing in Edinburgh over 'a pint o' wine'.

To be at the heart of Robert Burns is to be at the heart of what it is to be Scottish.

Go fetch to me a pint o wine,
    And fill it in a silver tassie;
That I may drink, before I go,
    A service to my bonie lassie:
The boat rocks at the Pier o Leith,
    Fu' loud the wind blaws frae the Ferry,
The ship rides by the Berwick-law,
    And I maun leave my bonie Mary.

The Silver Tassie

Robbie Shepherd

Broadcaster

And weary, o'er the muir, his course does hameward bend.

I first started to appreciate the works of Robert Burns as a loon about fourteen, when on a Hogmanay nicht, I would be first-footin' with my folks and listening to the local butcher singing the 'The Lea Rig'!

The words and music were to stay in my mind, leading me to pick up the family Burns book, and two or three years later I made my debut at a Burns Supper reciting *Tam o' Shanter* in the wee hall at the Lyne of Skene. I found it a very easy poem to learn: it was a continuous story, even if it took about twelve minutes to deliver.

Easy? Aye, until I started to accept other invitations, and it was at a Burns Supper in Huntly that a veteran o' sic affairs, sitting next to me, ventured to suggest, in agreeing with the ease in learning the words, that there were only two stanzas that might trip me up in full flight. They were the references to the storms, when 'the wind blew as 'twad blawn its last; the rattling showers rose on the blast', to be echoed a verse or two later when 'the doubling storm roars thro' the woods'.

You've guessed it, I stood up that night and got them the wrong way round, thereby shortening the tale, and to this day, I still have to concentrate on the weather warnings.

But my choice takes me away from what was a brilliant, theatrical, dramatic poem to one you seldom hear at a Burns Supper, maybe because the drams ream in owre mony noddles to fully appreciate it. It's *The Cotter's Saturday Night,* and though a hundred and fifty years on from then, it has me at my own family home mony a time, the cares of tomorrow gone as Dad finished yet another long day at work and the family circle were together for a wee while.

Burns paints such a bonnie picture of the breadwinner, the trauchl'd cotter, making his weary way home o'er the moor wi' the comforting thought o' his lonely cot, settling doon by the wee bit ingle, blinkan bonilie, having been greeted by the thrifty wifie's smile and the expectant wee things. Nae newspapers, wireless or TV tae soothe his achin' body.

The big ha'-Bible, 'ance his Father's pride', maybe didna feature in our house, but I still look back in awe at the one we had that belonged to Granny, with the muckle metal clasp and blank pages to write reverently on family matters. Aye, the link tae Burns is but a short trip as time goes by.

The poem is a brilliant insight into the life of the times, a complete social commentary, and ranks aside a' the bonnie rhyming words o' sweet romance he excelled in, including some of my favourite lines, written to Nancy McLehose on her departure for Jamaica in 1791, 'Had we never lov'd sae kindly,/ Had we never lov'd sae blindly'.

No, it has to be *The Cotter's Saturday Night,* as nae painter o the highest renown could have captured ony better the very essence of contentment.

Long may thy hardy sons of rustic toil
Be blest with health and peace and sweet content.

A lesson in there for us all.

There, lanely by the ingle-cheek
I sat an ey'd the spewing reek,
That fill'd, wi hoast-provoking smeek,
    The auld clay biggin;
An heard the restless rattons squeak
    About the riggin.

The Vision

Lesley Riddoch

Broadcaster and Writer

My Banffshire-born dad, Bill Riddoch, was a huge fan of Scottish poetry. As a result, I could recite 'The Puddock' by J. M. Caie at the age of 7. Sadly, where we lived in Belfast, not many people fully appreciated my Doric party piece. But everyone appreciated Robert Burns – and as a member of the Belfast Burns speaking circuit, Dad was in great demand.

Naturally, nothing adults did could possibly interest us as children. But watching your father sneak out dressed in a nightshirt and slippers, clutching a candle and nightcap, was different. Turned out there had been a bombing in Belfast that night, and the roadblocks and chaos that always followed meant uncertain arrival times – even at city centre venues normally just ten minutes' drive away. We assumed Dad was off to some strange adult fancy dress party – of course he was simply off to deliver 'Holy Wullie's Prayer'.

Burns was a huge part of Dad's life – and has accidentally become part of his afterlife. When he died suddenly, I sifted through his notebooks and discovered one of the last things he had written before leaving on holiday with Mum (he died while out for his daily jog in Majorca) was this…

> Is there a man, whose judgment clear,
> Can others teach the course to steer,
> Yet runs, himself, life's mad career,
>   Wild as the wave,
> Here pause – and, thro' the starting tear,
>   Survey this grave.

This seemed so apt we had the verse mounted on Dad's gravestone. But the monumental sculptor couldn't fit each line across the stone, and as a result the verse spilled over each line by one word. The result – a mass of text. A gravestone like a spider's web of words, filled from top to bottom with Burns – my dad's name just managing to slip in.

Actually, like every Burns poem you think about for more than a few minutes, the haphazard, scattered appearance of the verse conveyed its message about the ultimate futility of 'man's dominion' very well. And for a man who used up more than nine lives as a fighter pilot during the Second World War – it accidentally fitted my Dad very well too.

I inherited a lot of Dad's interests, and an original set of William Paterson's six-volume *Works of Robert Burns*, so old and apparently untouched that clumps of pages were uncut at the margins and had to be turned in folded clumps – or cut carefully to reveal their contents. It was a treasure chest, with every surviving letter Burns sent and received including this, his last letter written on 12 July 1796:

'After all my boasted independence, curst Necessity compounds me to implore you for five pounds. A cruel scoundrel of a Haberdasher, to whom I owe an account, taking it into his head that I am dying, has commenced a process, and will infallibly put me into jail. Do, for God's sake, send me that sum and that by return of post. Forgive me this earnestness; but the horrors of a jail have made me half distracted. I do not ask all this gratuitously; upon returning health I hereby promise and engage to furnish you with five pounds worth of the neatest song genius you have ever seen.'

It's been part of Scotland's tragedy that great creative genius has been crippled because of small material wants. And it's our job to change that – inspired by his optimism, generosity of spirit and courtesy – in the face of every unfairness life had to fling his way.

O ye, whose cheek the tear of pity stains,
    Draw near with pious reverence and attend!
Here lie the loving husband's dear remains,
    The tender father, and the generous friend:
The pitying heart that felt for human wo!
    The dauntless heart that fear'd no human pride!
The friend of man, to vice alone a foe,
    "For ev'n his failings lean'd to virtue's side".

For the Author's Father, Alloway Kirk

Shirley Bell

Chief Executive of the Robert Burns World Federation

Touched by Robert Burns is a most appropriate name for this publication by Andy Hall.

The works of the Bard have certainly touched the heart of many, and provide a catalyst for people to come together in the spirit of friendship. This is evidenced by the many Burns Clubs and vast number of Suppers that take place in celebration of the birth of Robert Burns. Many who leave their native land take with them a most important piece of luggage – their Scottish culture – and this ensures the influence of Robert Burns and his works on people from around the globe.

The following is a small sample of an extensive list of many prominent individuals who have written of their admiration for the poet.

Abraham Lincoln: 'I cannot frame a toast to Burns; I can say nothing worthy of his generous heart and transcending genius.'

William Wordsworth: 'The poet [Burns] writes under one restriction only, namely, the necessity of giving immediate pleasure to a human being.'

John Ruskin: 'The books that have most influenced me are – Coleridge and Keats in my youth, Burns as I grew older and wiser.'

Ogden Nash: 'Burns wrote like an angel and lived like a man.'

Sir Arthur Conan Doyle: 'Burns is supreme in the qualities of the heart.'

Goethe: 'Burns is amongst the first poetical spirits which the past century has produced.'

Lord Byron: 'The rank of Burns is the very first of his art.'

Andrew Carnegie: 'The longer I live, the more I appreciate Burns as a man and a Poet…'

William Ewart Gladstone: 'His works bear impressed upon them, beyond the possibility of mistake, the stamp of genius.'

John Ramsay of Ochtertyre: 'I have been in the company of many men of genius, some of them poets; but never witnessed such flashes of intellectual brightness as from him, the impulse of a moment – flashes of celestial fire.'

Lord Rosebery: 'Burns had honour in his lifetime, but his fame has rolled like a snowball since his death and it rolls on.'

The tributes paid by these illustrious gentlemen demonstrate the genius that is Robert Burns, and any further contribution I might attempt would seem paltry by comparison; however I feel that I have shared his life through his poetry, songs and writings, and empathise with his philosophies.

Since joining the Robert Burns World Federation, I have had the privilege of meeting people from many lands and all walks of life. Lasting friendships have been established and the warm hospitality afforded by strangers is extraordinary and most welcome.

Those of us touched by the works of Robert Burns have a responsibility to pass to the next generation the tremendous legacy left in his treasure chest of words, and that is why the Robert Burns World Federation is at the forefront of promoting school competitions in the disciplines of poetry, music, art and singing, which each year attract 160,000 children. This is a story worth telling, and that is why I continue to support the work of our worldwide organisation.

Gie me ae spark o Nature's fire,
That's a' the learning I desire;
Then, tho' I drudge thro dub an mire
At pleugh or cart,
My Muse, tho hamely in attire,
May touch the heart.

Epistle to J. Lapraik

Karine Polwart

Songwriter/Singer

When I was twenty-one, the shrunken body of my lovely Grampa, Peter Quinn, finally gave out for good. The evening before his funeral, a friend dropped through my letterbox a tape called *Handful of Earth* by a singer I'd never heard of before, called Dick Gaughan.

Well, the emotional intensity of that album blew me away, and it remains one of my all-time favourites to this day. In particular, it includes a version of 'Now Westlin Winds' that's as moving a performance of a Burns song as I think I'll ever hear, and indeed one of the most powerful and poignant songs in any genre that I've heard yet. With its gorgeous dense natural imagery and its musing upon the myriad ways in which we human beings inhabit the landscape of this world, it manages to say something intimate and huge at the same time. It's a love song and a massive metaphysical statement too, and made me realise for the first time that Burns was about so much more than waspish young girls with coy voices clasping their hands in gutless, Jean Brodie-esque renditions of 'Ca' the Yowes' at the annual school Burns song competition.

If 'Now Westlin Winds' started something for me that evening, then my Grampa's choice of 'Ae Fond Kiss' as the parting piece of ceremonial music at his funeral the following day nearly finished me off. Even played by an indifferent undertaker on a cheesy Casio keyboard, it socked me right in the belly that morning. Though I'd sung that song to myself countless times, indeed it was one of the few songs I'd ever sung in public too, 'ae fareweel, alas, for ever' took on an entirely different meaning for me in that moment. And that's the thing about a truly great song, that it's big enough and spacious enough to accommodate a thousand meanings and never lose its relevance. And Burns has dozens and dozens of those songs. It's remarkable.

There are other personal connections – my dad opened my own wedding ceremony with 'My Luve's like a Red, Red Rose' – but as a songwriter myself, my enthusiasm is deeper and wider than that. I'm the same age now as Burns was when he died. To consider what he created in that short life makes me aspire for just one ounce of the empathy of 'The Slave's Lament' or 'My Tocher's the Jewel', the earthiness of 'Wee Willie Gray' or 'Brose and Butter', the wit of 'Holy Willie's Prayer' or the wisdom of 'A Man's a Man for A' That'; and the same length of time again with which to create a single song that might speak to someone else the way so many of his songs speak to me.

But a' the pleasures e'er I saw,
    Tho three times doubl'd fairly –
That happy night was worth them a',
    Amang the rigs o' barley.

The Rigs o' Barley

Pat Nevin

Former Footballer, Journalist, Football Analyst

In terms of understanding, learning and enjoying the works of Burns, I have been something of a late convert. Certainly Burns was not taught to any level at my school, and considering I went on to do Sixth Year Studies in English, it is almost impossible to comprehend that oversight now.

Many who haven't been brought up with Burns' work, and go on to appreciate it, find the beauty in it following on from a growing interest in their history and culture as they grow older and try to understand themselves. Others have an epiphany at one of the many Burns suppers that have become an ever-growing feature of Scottish life, though the quantity of alcohol can have a positive and negative effect on these occasions.

Although both of the above affected me, it was a third entry point that finally brought a clearer understanding of the beauty and brilliance of our greatest poet. It was the music that has been created to frame his work.

There have been many artists who have been moved to add tunes of their own to the more classical renditions we have grown to love. The folk music tradition in Scotland has always been lively, but recently new takes have been added which have updated the sound without losing the soul of the works, and sometimes even adding something totally new.

Some years ago, Eddi Reader released 'Ae Fond Kiss' soon after her phenomenal mainstream pop success with the band Fairground Attraction. It introduced Burns to an audience who otherwise would have had little opportunity to hear the poetry and little interest in translating or understanding the words.

In Scotland now there are huge crossovers in the music scene from folk to the rock, pop and indie genres. Younger audiences are delighted with a real alternative to the overproduced plastic sounds being churned out to order from down south and over the pond. When these offerings are backed up with truly wonderful lyrics by Robert Burns, the results can be magical.

The Delgados were for many years the doyens of the Scottish music scene, and they recorded a fine version of 'A Parcel of Rogues', but there have been many others. Another recent case in point, and my particular favourite, is the young Glasgow band Camera Obscura. They were asked by the late John Peel to provide a session for his Burns Night show. Their takes on 'Ae Fond Kiss', 'Cock Up Your Beaver' and 'Red, Red Rose' were charming, but their rendition of 'Love My Jean', was so impressive that it was released as a single, and was for many people, including me, one of the best singles of the year of any genre, as well as one of the most beautiful renditions of Burns I have ever heard.

The John Peel show itself had a year-end chart voted for by the listeners, and 'Love My Jean' was voted in at Number 7 in 2005. Considering this was an audience that has interests in innovative music from hardcore dance to thrash punk, the power of Burns allied to a beautiful tune, and, it has to be said, an equally beautiful voice, made it a breakthrough moment for many.

I can think of few better ways to enjoy Burns than to listen to his words sung beautifully, while looking at images which remind you of his life and times, with maybe a wee whisky to accompany it.

Scotland, my auld, respected mither!
Tho whiles ye moistify your leather,
Till whare ye sit on craps o heather,
Ye tine your dam;
Freedom an whisky gang thegither
Tak aff your dram!

The Author's Earnest Cry and Prayer to the Scotch Representatives in
the House of Commons

Richard Thompson

Singer/Songwriter with Fairport Convention

My father was the classic exile. Recruited from the Scottish Borders by the London police a few years before World War Two, his roots soon became precious to him, and there was no possible way that he was going to dilute his heritage by being in a 'foreign' country. His shelves were lined with Walter Scott, his turntable hummed to Jimmy Shand, and he never missed a Burns Night.

For me, growing up in post-war, pre-satire London was pretty dull in terms of entertainment – one TV channel (two eventually), and dread holes in the radio scheduling (The Sunday Teatime of the Soul). Out of boredom, I'd pick books off the shelf, and soon found myself reading the Waverley novels, books of Border ballads, and the collected works of Burns. This was, of course, a great way to atone for my various sins in the eyes of my father who, if he caught me taking a peek at anything of the Bard's, would regale me with a twenty-stanza party piece from *Tam o' Shanter* and give me an approving pat on the head.

None of this seemed very relevant as the Beatles and Brigitte Bardot and *Private Eye* changed my world, and Howlin' Wolf and John Coltrane were on the front burner. But as I began to write songs, it was instinctively the old Scottish bones that I tried to put new flesh on, and when my band, Fairport Convention, decided to ditch the transatlantic influences and to play music built on British roots, it was like a homecoming, and I had new appreciation of Burns the songwriter.

Why was he a great songwriter? He was a lyrics-only man – as far as I know, he always used existing traditional tunes – but his words are eminently singable. There is no pretension in his songs; there is none of the artifice of a W.H. Auden writing for Stravinsky's *Rake's Progress*, none of the intellectual and artistic sense of superiority that a poet sometimes feels he has to thrust insensitively upon the singer and the listener. Burns wrote in a natural language that sat easily upon the music and the tongue, and the proof of his art is the body of work – hundreds of fine songs – that are sung every day around the world. He would be in my all-time UK top ten of songwriters – up there with Lennon and McCartney, Ewan McColl, Lady Nairn, Elvis Costello, Lal Waterson, George Bruce Thompson…

My father remained a Burns devotee. During the whole later part of his life, he only missed one Burns Supper – he died on January 25th, 1992.

Flow gently, sweet Afton, among thy green braes!
Flow gently, sweet river, the theme of my lays!
My Mary's asleep by thy murmuring stream –
Flow gently, sweet Afton, disturb not her dream!

Sweet Afton

Denis Lawson

Actor

My earliest association with Robert Burns was when I was eight years old and I won the 'Burns Prize' at school for reciting one of his poems 'Up in the Morning Early', which began 'Up in the morning's no for me.' Frankly, at that age it could have been written for me!

I hasten to add this was merely within the class, so it was modest by any standards, but since I was never a prizewinner at school in any area, it was a big day for me!

Apart from that I'd cite 'Ae Fond Kiss' as my favourite love song bar none, and *Tam o' Shanter*, a piece that's crammed with extraordinary writing and images that you can almost touch and smell.

I also take great comfort that Burns' handwriting was quite appalling: it's almost as bad as mine.

Now, do thy speedy utmost, Meg,
And win the key-stane of the brig;
There, at them thou thy tail may toss,
A running stream they dare na cross!

Tam o' Shanter

Michael Marra

Singer/Songwriter

It's an ill wind…

When I was fourteen years old I attended, intermittently, Lawside Academy which, by then, was situated near St Mary's in the frozen north of Dundee.

One morning, while reeling from two mind-numbing periods of mathematics, we were told that our English teacher was indisposed and that we were to make our way to Mr Ferrie's room instead. I had seen Mr Ferrie around the school and he seemed like a cheery, good-natured man, but we had never been subjected to him as a teacher.

My usual fear and dread lifted when he told us he would read a poem by Robert Burns. What followed was wonderful, because he didn't just read it, he produced a superb performance of *Tam o' Shanter* while playing a recording of Malcolm Arnold's music inspired by the piece. I believe that there was not a boy in that class who wasn't captivated by his display of acting skills, his relish for the language and most of all his love for every syllable of the epic work. Love is the word. Here was a man with a noble purpose, he was excited and thrilled to be introducing us to the jewels of a giant who had been born among us.

His performance discarded the need for thirty or forty questions about the text that would have wasted our time had we been looking at the page rather than associating a word with a facial expression. He could have been an actor – I've worked with worse – but he was a great teacher armed with superior material, and he had what was usually a riot of fourteen-year-old boys in his thrall.

The next time I looked in my father's *Kilmarnock Edition* it didn't look like German as it had before, and I have regarded Burns' work with professional envy ever since. I love the fact that Robert considered himself a songwriter, and regret the fact that his political work has been ignored in practice. Elsewhere, a song like 'A Man's a Man' could have led a revolution.

> Think! ye may buy the joys o'er dear,
> Remember Tam o' Shanter's mare.

Now rosy May comes in wi flowers
To deck her gay, green-spreading bowers;
And now comes in the happy hours
To wander wi my Davie.

Dainty Davie

Christine Kydd

Traditional Singer and Contemporary Songwriter

What folksinger in Scotland could say their life and work had not been influenced in some way by the writing and collecting of Robert Burns? As children at school in Glasgow we heard his poems in the school hall with 'something called the Burns Federation'. The strains of 'Ye Banks and Braes o' Bonnie Doon' could be heard right down the corridor as the whole class sang along to the BBC Schools Radio programme 'Singing Together', and 'hey look! that guy that did those "pomes" and this song as well – look – his song is here! Alongside all the *English* songs and songs from lots of countries as well, and it's Scottish and people think it's good!' Even though it was taught in English, we didn't really notice. It's a song I still sing in concerts, now of course in Scots, and I love it even more now than I did in Primary 7.

A little book about food in the days of Robert Burns fascinated me – the crops, the cattle, and how they used every part of the beast ('they had a thing like black pudding then?') This early interest in social history has influenced me, and led me to my current study of folklore.

Young adult life took me to Edinburgh. Rod Paterson's singing of Burns inspired me hugely. Glasgow's Tramway Theatre (City of Culture 1990) hosted *Jock Tamson's Bairns*, a fantastic theatre show by Communicado. I was delighted to be involved in the show, singing with Rod and what was to become the Cauld Blast Orchestra. With Burns as a theme, the show incorporated song, music, dance and theatre. 'Gloomy December', 'Song Composed in August', 'Wantonness' were just a few of the songs. Later I sang with Janet Russell, Chantan, and now solo and with Sinsheen.

There is rarely a concert set which doesn't include at least one of his songs – 'The Slave's Lament', 'Duncan Gray', 'The Dusty Miller', 'Siller Tassie'. It's the connection with real life and real people, human nature, the blood and guts, as well as the finer and cultured aspects of his work that really speak to me. The well-observed 'Holy Willie's Prayer', or the drama of *Tam o' Shanter*.

At this point I stop to consider, but I just can't resist telling you that I discovered a family connection! My great granny Isabella Crabb Burness links me to his forebears in the Mearns, and it looks like I'm a relative (extremely distant). I can't help feeling honoured, however tentative the link.

And then, 'Auld Lang Syne'! Isn't it amazing that this wee country spawned that iconic international song which celebrates the fact that neither time nor tide can spoil the enduring nature of friendship? Whatever you might think of the man or portrayals of his lifestyle, surely you can't ignore the ability of his work to inspire. From poetry, recitation and song on the printed page, to the contemporary recordings of his songs by Jean Redpath (Greentrax), or the fabulous *Songs of Robert Burns* (Linn) featuring a whole range of great Scottish singers, Burns' works will provide inspiration for years to come. It's impossible to sum up the breadth of his artistic contribution to our culture – lyricism, humour, poetry, romance, bawdiness and social commentary.

Robert Burns, a man raised in Scotland, speaks to us still, over a couple of centuries later, in a contemporary voice, and has touched the hearts and minds of people all over the world. I'm very glad to be one of them.

The braes ascend like lofty wa's,
The foaming stream, deep-roaring, fa's
O'erhung wi fragrant-spreading shaws,
The birks of Aberfeldie.

The Birks of Aberfeldie

Ferenc Szasz

Professor of History, University of New Mexico

Like many Americans of my generation, I grew to maturity surrounded by the phrases of Robert Burns. I discovered the hard way that 'the best laid schemes o' mice an' men/Gang aft agley', and always hoped that 'O wad some Pow'r the giftie gie us/To see oursels as others see us!' And along with most of my countrymen, every December 31st I joined in singing 'Auld Lang Syne'. These passages, along with Burns' classic comment 'A man's a man for a' that', have long been woven into American English, although I suspect that few people could trace their origin to a famed Ayrshire ploughman.

Still, I never really comprehended Burns' impact on the United States until 1991/92, when my wife, Margaret, and I spent a year on a teaching exchange at the University of Aberdeen. While researching on the subject of 'Scotland and the American Civil War', I discovered that Abraham Lincoln had often said that Robert Burns was his favourite poet. During his youth in Indiana and Illinois, Lincoln memorized many of Burns' verses, including *Tam o' Shanter*, 'Holy Willie's Prayer' and 'The Cotter's Saturday Night'. And just days before his assassination in April of 1865, he recited the last verses of 'Lament for James, Earl of Glencairn' to his secretary John Hay.

Why did the foremost historical figure of the United States hold the foremost literary figure of Scotland in such high esteem? As I pored through Burns' collected poems and letters, the parallels slowly began to emerge: both men came from poor farming families that often barely kept the wolf from the door. Both had minimal formal schooling, but clearly understood the core of human nature. And both left a legacy of the written word that has echoed through time for over two hundred years.

Given this overlap, it is perhaps no accident that twelve American cities – including New York, Albany, Denver and Cheyenne – have erected heroic statues to Burns, or that in 1893 Scotland became the first nation outside the United States to erect a similar statue to Lincoln, one that stands today in the Old Calton Hill Burial Ground in Edinburgh.

Although Burns and Lincoln never met, they shared a similar world view: each rejected entrenched privilege, scorned hypocrisy, and drew heavily from a biblical, rather than a denominational, religious perspective. And each voiced confidence in the intrinsic worth of the ordinary person. Both men saw the *quest* for equality as the highest social goal.

How has Robert Burns touched my life? I became so fascinated with his impact on Abraham Lincoln that I wrote a book linking the two men.

The Statue of Robert Burns in Dumfries town centre

The statue was carved in Tuscany by Italian craftsmen working to a model by Amelia Hill. It was unveiled by the Earl of Rosebery on 6 April 1882

Shirley Spear

Chef and Owner of the Three Chimneys, Skye

Miss Bullen was sharp. A neat woman with a well-shaped sixties haircut, she was petite with an angular frame. She was always a sharp dresser, choosing close-fitting short skirts, perhaps a twinset or ribbed, roll-neck sweater and, naturally, pointy shoes with clicky heels. With her long-fingered, bony hands, she waved us into song on the downbeat and immediately proceeded to accompany us on the upright piano, the keys clicking through the notes in sharp time.

I was never sure if I liked Miss Bullen. I never felt a rapport with her, but I can still feel the childlike sense of awe I had about her ability to command, control and cajole the whole class through our weekly singing lessons. I loved those brusque, half-hour classes in the room upstairs. This room was also where I painstakingly learned to knit and sew, left-handed and slower than anyone else in the class. Singing my heart out to Miss Bullen's nimble fingers tripping over the piano keys was a great deal more fun.

Clutching our copies of the school songbook, we all turned obediently to the correct page. And then, the strict learning process began; note by note, bar by bar, phrase by phrase, quavers and dotted crotchets were dealt with precisely. I remember all the tunes as well as many of the words. We sang songs like 'The Four Marys', 'Gossip Joan', 'Rowan Tree', 'The Piper o' Dundee' and, of course, those by Robert Burns. Those songs will be in my head for all time. They are impossible to forget. Songs such as 'My Heart's in the Highlands', 'Coming thro' the Rye', 'Flow Gently Sweet Afton', 'Ca' the Yowes to the Knowes' and the joyous 'Charlie He's My Darling'. A rousing chorus from this page in the book always got the class singing together with great cheer, obviously quickening Miss Bullen's heart as the crescendo rose towards her final staccato chord.

She would snap shut the piano lid in a defining gesture to signal the end of her lesson, and meekly, we filed out of the room upstairs, back to our main classroom. Singing with Miss Bullen was over for another week.

I was probably always in a class of around forty boys and girls throughout my primary school years at South Morningside in Edinburgh. I loved school, relishing every day of fun and great friendship. Competing for the annual Burns' prize for poetry meant learning one of the Bard's poems by heart, practising meticulous pronunciation of all the tongue-twisting words of true Scots. I would rehearse for hours at home, putting as much 'expression' (as my Mother called it) into every line, to prove that I understood it all.

My Mother wrote beautiful poetry in her schooldays and loved to read it. She won prizes for her writing and even had it published in the *Scotsman*. She could recite verses from all manner of poets' work. This poetic gene ran through older members of her family, and needless to say, learning the works of Robert Burns was always encouraged with great zeal. This was something I shone at – and probably loved the attention it brought me as one of a family of five!

Many years later, here in the midst of the Isle of Skye's academic storm of staunch Gaelic revival, an Elgin-born neighbour of mine used to organise a traditional Burns Supper in Dunvegan. Henry Steven was a past master of the Toast to the Lassies. The year I was invited to present the reply, Charles Kennedy, our MP, was guest of honour. Brian Wilson, ex-Editor of the local *West Highland Free Press,* but by then, rapidly attaining great heights at Westminster, delivered the Immortal Memory. What a night we had! In a style true to my Mother's indelible sense of occasion, I relished the importance of my role that evening and spent days preparing my address in rhyming couplets, using her little blue book of the *Works* that I rescued from her belongings when she died. I aimed to shine on her behalf – and on behalf of the national Bard's great language too. My inheritance prevailed!

Edina! Scotia's darling seat!
All hail thy palaces and tow'rs,
Where once, beneath a Monarch's feet,
Sat Legislation's sov'reign pow'rs.

Address to Edinburgh

Duncan Bruce

Writer

It is very easy for me to describe how the works of Robert Burns have touched my life: he has made this born American a Scot. It is true that three of my grandparents were born in Scotland, two of them Presbyterians, and some might think that is background enough to establish my identity. But if you were to visit the Pittsburgh neighbourhood where I grew up, you would find that we Scots were lost in an ethnic sea of over forty different European groups among our six thousand inhabitants.

Some of us were of Scottish descent, but were assimilated and didn't stand out as being very different from the rest, and there were many non-Scottish-Americans who were Presbyterians.

What defined me and my family most as Scots were the poems and songs of Burns. I doubt if there were more then a few in the neighbourhood who would ever even have heard of Burns or have known one of his lyrics. But by the time I grew to be fifteen, I could sing and play on the piano songs like 'Duncan Gray', 'Afton Water', 'Comin' thro' the Rye' and 'Corn Rigs Are Bonnie'.

Much later in life I met an old man, a Scottish immigrant, who was dying in a nursing home in New York City where I live. He had asked to meet me entirely because a friend had told him that I was a Scot, and the old man wanted to meet someone who was 'one of his people' before he died.

He lay on his back in the bed, unable to move any part of his body except for his beautiful blue eyes and his broad mouth. Immediately, he asked me if I knew any Burns, and both of us started singing and quoting the bard. The old man smiled, and I asked him if he thought Burns to be the best poet of all time. 'Undoubtedly', was his only remark.

And so it is that we who are Scottish are so affected by the works of Robert Burns. Some people think that he created Scottish ways, but I think it is just the opposite. Burns told us what we had already defined as Scottish: things such as 'A man's a man for a' that' and 'An honest man's the noblest work of God'.

Burns knew what the Scottish virtues were and how they made us Scottish. He told us, in beautiful dialect, who we were, and why we were different, and he did it far better than anyone else.

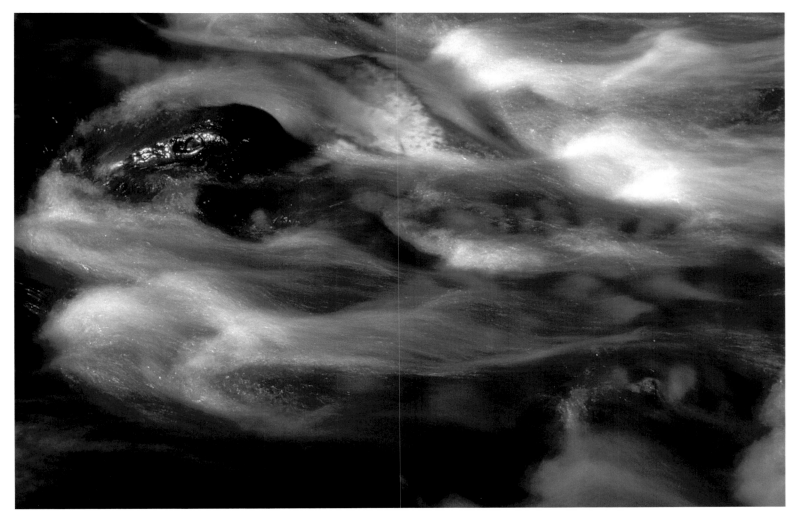

Thy crystal stream, Afton, how lovely it glides,
And winds by the cot where my Mary resides!
How wanton thy waters her snowy feet lave,
As, gathering sweet flowerets, she stems thy clear wave!

Sweet Afton

Cameron McNeish

Writer, Broadcaster, Mountaineer

The natural miracle of hydrodynamics is best observed in very wet weather conditions, when our moors and mountains harness all the fallen rain, soak it up like a gargantuan sponge, then, by unseen energies, force it up though the surface of the ground in the form of bubbling streams. The Bruar Water, just north of Blair Atholl, feeds from the great soggy plateaux and moors of upper Atholl and, initially, flows gently down the empty miles of Glen Bruar before, chameleon-like, changing character completely.

As the ground falls away, the waters become agitated and turbulent, before crashing and thundering down the deep gorge that cradles its bed. At the foot of the gorge, the water roars over a series of falls and cascades before finally surging through a natural arch in the rock and into the pools below. The river is at its finest during and immediately after periods of heavy rain – that's the best time to view the aquatic power of these Bruar Falls.

What makes Bruar so spectacular is the simple combination of rock, water and trees, basic elements that offer grandeur on a magnificent scale; but in the late eighteenth century this narrow glen was virtually devoid of trees. One visitor to the falls, William Gilpin, commented, 'One of them indeed is a grand fall, but it is so naked in its accompaniments that it is of little value.'

But it was Robert Burns, in 1787, who was responsible for changing the character of this beauty spot. He wasn't all that impressed with the place, and later wrote 'The Humble Petition of Bruar Water to the Noble Duke of Athole.'

This eleven-verse poem contains the lines, 'Would then my noble master please/ To grant my highest wishes?/ He'll shade my banks wi' towering trees,/ And bonnie spreading bushes.'

The Duke of Atholl acquiesced, and the first trees were planted in 1797. Sadly, the Bard died before the plantations grew, but others have left their impressions in words and pictures – William Wordsworth, William Turner, Queen Victoria and thousands of appreciative visitors from home and abroad.

Whenever I pass through Atholl, I'm reminded of the influence of the ploughman-poet. Generations of Dukes of Atholl have planted trees in and around the area, indeed the woodlands of Atholl are one of the rich characteristics of the region, and it's probably amongst the best wooded areas of the highlands.

I wonder what Atholl would be like today if Robert Burns hadn't felt the need to advise the mighty laird on how to improve his property. The power of simple verse changed attitudes and an entire landscape. We have a lot to thank Robert Burns for, and not just his wonderful legacy of song and verse.

Here, foaming down the skelvy rocks,
In twisting strength I rin;
There high my boiling torrent smokes,
Wild-roaring o'er a linn.

The Humble Petition of Bruar Water to the Noble Duke of Athole

Tam White

Singer of Jazz and Blues

My earliest recollection of Robert Burns is sitting in front of an open-range fire in a single-end in a tenement building in The Pleasance, one of the main thoroughfares in the south side of Scotland's capital city, toasting bread and listening with my big sister Pearl to our Granny tell stories about a young man who left his home in Ayrshire and headed for what must have been the 'Bright Lights, Big City' of its day, the city of Edinburgh, 'Auld Reekie'.

During one of those long winter nights, our Grandmother told us about her brother-in-law, our great-uncle R. Murdoch, better known as Cantie Young, a professional runner/miner who, in his time, had been well-respected for his knowledge of the said poet and his works, and had given the Immortal Memory at many Burns Suppers throughout Scotland in the twenties and thirties.

She then went on to tell us about a mouse, an old grey mare called Meg, her master Tam o' Shanter and their ride home passing by the auld kirk where witches and warlocks were throwing a right auld shindig. It made us curl up in the chair and hide our faces, while still peeking through our fingers, making sure we wouldn't miss a trick.

My next step was to start learning the songs of Burns: 'Ae Fond Kiss', 'My Luve's Like a Red, Red Rose', and still remaining a favourite is 'Afton Water'. 'A Man's a Man' still stirs the soul, and 'Scots Wha Hae' was always a big favourite in Sandy Bell's pub on a Saturday night, but let's go back just a little.

I had started off my education at Castle Hill Primary School – as the name suggests, next door to Edinburgh's Castle. So it would seem that in all the places I played as a young boy, Burns had played himself, no doubt in different ways, but I'm sure with the same commitment.

There's a third connection that drew me ever closer to the man. I moved into my Grandfather's house, that was the same address that Burns stayed in on his last visit to Edinburgh, the White Hart Inn, 32 The Grassmarket, so as a young boy, strange but true, I always thought of him as a neighbour.

But on answering the question how much did Robert Burns influence myself and my music, although I was young and from a very different neck of the woods, it became apparent when I first heard the songs of Huddie Leadbetter (Leadbelly) and blues poets such as Big Bill Broonzy and Muddy Waters speaking about the same subjects with the same passion, I was hooked.

I'm not the first and I don't suppose I'll be the last to say that Burns was, and still is, undoubtedly, a true giant in the written word, and a man of the people.

> 'Oh Clarinda, can you hear me,
> Hear me calling out your name,
> Oh Clarinda, can you hear me,
> Sylvander cried in vain.'

There, watching high the least alarms,
Thy rough, rude fortress gleams afar;
Like some bold vet'ran, grey in arms,
And mark'd with many a seamy scar.

Address to Edinburgh

Andrew Weir

Actor

Growing up in Ayrshire with a grandmother who used phrases like: 'Ye'll dicht yer e'en mair than ye'll dicht yer mooth!' made being captivated by the use of auld Scots unavoidable; and in my opinion no one did more for our native tongue than Robert Burns.

Of course, my introduction to Burns went far beyond that. Anyone who has ever been to Ayr will surely have observed that there is just no way of ignoring the Bard and his work – his namesakes range from petrol stations to pubs and from hotels to chip-shops. As an Ayrshire schoolchild, if you hadn't toured Burns cottage at least five times by the age of 10, you must have had an extremely worrying sickness record.

I learned to speak Burns' verse around the same time that I learned to read, and at the age of seven, entered my first verse-speaking competition. With the immortal words 'Gie a' the faes o' Scotland's weal/ A towmond's toothache!' I won my first Ayrshire Burns Federation award, and from there I was hooked.

I can honestly say that everything I have done since then can, in no small part, be attributed to the simple pleasure of being allowed to perform in my accent, something that just felt right and that – in some inexplicable way – came naturally. This served not only as a confidence-booster for one of the least studious children in the class, but also as a point on which this excitable seven-year-old could focus. In many ways, it was through Burns' work that I learned how to live life, respect others and love my country.

In my work as an actor, I constantly called upon Burns' unique characterisation and phrasing to shape a role or present a monologue – even when performing Shakespeare! I now live and work in New York, and on my travels around the United States, I often find myself sharing a few lines of Burns, which offer timeless anecdotes and haunting reminders of how we should conduct ourselves and behave towards our fellow human beings. It is too often forgotten that Burns wrote of humanitarian issues and equal rights around 150 years before it was fashionable or socially acceptable to do so.

As poverty and 'man's inhumanity to man' continue to devastate, I often think of how profound Burns' words, 'The honest man, though e'er sae poor,/ Is king o' men for a' that' really are.

When I backpacked around the world in 2003, it was always flattering to hear that a movie, in which I had played a very small part, had joined golf and whisky as one of those instantly recognisable icons of Scotland. It wasn't *Braveheart*, however, that gave me the biggest patriotic thrill, but once again – Burns. I had hired a motorbike tour guide in Cambodia's capital city, Phnom Penh. His name was Jack Thy, he was around the same age as me, had an encyclopaedic knowledge of his country and worked for around $2 a day. As we toured some of the sites, Jack had to stop his bike and take a call from another customer looking to take a tour. It was his ring-tone of choice that interested me – 'Auld Lang Syne', and he even knew all of the words!

At dawn, when every grassy blade
Droops with a diamond at his head;
At ev'n, when beans their fragrance shed,
        I' th' rustling gale;
Ye maukins, whidden thro the glade,
        Come join my wail!

Elegy on Captain Matthew Henderson

Frieda Morrison

Broadcaster/Musician

That was the deal – my travelling companion, Cliff Jones, wanted to see the simian fox in the Ethiopian Highlands, and I wanted to find the Lost Ark of the Covenant in the north of Ethiopia. We would accompany each other.

We had been travelling through quite a few countries together, over the last year, making programmes about sustainable tourism for BBC Radio Scotland, and the Ethiopian programme was the last in the series. We had no luck with the fox, but it was a great trip, past the falls of the Blue Nile. So now it was the turn of the Ark, which I had heard was in Axum on the borders of Eritrea. Axum was just a short trip away by plane from the small airport at Lalibela in the Central Highlands. If only the plane would arrive; it was due four hours ago, and the temperature was rising.

Imagine the scene, then. There I was, with my companions Cliff and Habtamu Bekel, our wonderful guide – mothers outside feeding their babies… and a goat or donkey and some cattle wander periodically across the runway, chased by a man blowing a whistle. And still no sign of the plane. Suddenly, over the Tannoy comes a surprising but somewhat familiar sound – me singing 'Ae Fond Kiss' by Robert Burns. Cliff Jones had my CD stashed in his bag, and had managed to get the manager to play it over the airport system – surreal or what? – in the middle of Ethiopia. A more surreal moment was yet to come.

I should mention that as well as being an expert on all things Natural History, Mr Jones is also very knowledgeable about aeroplanes, having been in the RAF during the last war. This talent comes in handy, I'm sure, sometimes. On this occasion, I don't know if I appreciated his wisdom.

As we came in to land in Axum, he gently leaned across the chair in the cramped little plane and quietly whispered in his broad Lancashire accent, 'I would hold on tight, pet – that engine on the left isn't too good and he's coming in a bit fast to the runway.' We had been through quite a few hair-raising moments on our travels together, but this was scary. I started to quietly sing 'Ae Fond Kiss'. Mr Jones, who was the pillar of his local church choir, started to hum the tune. We landed with a puncture on impact and the accompanying skids and twirls, bangs and thumps.

But we made it, and made it to the end of 'Ae Fond Kiss'. We even made it to the Lost Ark, but that's another story.

The bauld Pitcur fell in a furr,
An Clavers gat a clankie, O,
Or I had fed an Athole gled,
On the braes o Killiecrankie, O!

Killicrankie

Tony Roper

Writer

In 1975, I was on a tour of the United States of America with a variety show about Scotland. It starred Alastair McDonald, Isla St Clair, a host of highly talented musicians, dancers and me. I was the actor, whose task it was to provide something different from the music side of the evening. This I did by means of a couple of comic monologues and two of Robert Burns' better known poems. The first was 'My Luve's like a Red, Red Rose', which, admittedly, is a song, but I recited it while a violin played the melody in the background. The second was 'A Man's a Man', which remains my favourite to this day.

We toured the States north, south, east and west, and always we were received enthusiastically. It is, however, one night in particular that stands out in my memory. We were in a small town in Alabama, and the night was going as well as ever, so I did not envisage any untoward reaction when I stepped on stage and gave an intro to 'A Man's a Man'.

This went along the lines of 'Robert Burns never bowed the knee to anyone. It was his firm conviction that we were all brothers and sisters, no matter their race, creed or colour.' As I uttered that last word, there was an audible intake of breath from the audience, and I could not only feel, but almost touch the tension that my words had evoked. I was, I don't mind admitting, more than a bit unnerved.

Then I thought to myself, this is precisely the type of gathering that made Burns write this poem, and I launched into it with all the fervour I could muster. I would like to say that when I finished it the audience rose as one and gave thunderous applause. Alas, no!

The approval, however, no longer mattered to me. I had been offered the opportunity to really live what the poet felt, and I revelled doing the poem more that night, at that time in Alabama's history, than on any other, and my pride in being a kinsman of Robert Burns has remained with me till the present.

Now simmer blinks on flow'ry braes,
And o'er the crystal streamlets plays,
Come let us spend the lightsome days
In the birks of Aberfeldie!

The Birks of Aberfeldie

Rod Paterson

Musician

Anyone who has witnessed, in the autumn gloaming, the astonishing formation stunt-flying of swallows, in rehearsal for their journey to Africa, will know exactly what Burns meant when he wrote in 'Now Westlin Winds',

> But, Peggy dear, the ev'ning's clear,
> Thick flies the skimming swallow.

Bogjorgan, Glenbervie, Kincardineshire
home of Walter Burness and Isobel Greig, great-great-grandparents of Robert Burns. Walter died at Bogjorgan in November 1670.

Fiona Kennedy

Singer

One of the many wonderful things about the legacy of Robert Burns is how he and his work continue to touch the hearts and minds of people all over the world. There are no annual dinners for Tolstoy, Shakespeare or Brecht, but Burns lives on powerfully through his wondrous poetry and song, much of it as relevant today as it ever was.

How true the words and message remain of 'A Man's a Man for A' That', and how right it was that this was sung at the opening of Scotland's Parliament.

As a Kennedy, our family seat is the eighteenth-century Culzean Castle, in Burns country, not too far away from Souter Johnnie's Cottage. Culzean is a glorious, romantic place with magnificent views over the River Clyde and the architect Robert Adam's final masterpiece. It has very special and happy memories for me, as my 'Uncle' Jimmy Logan had a flat there where we often stayed and visited as a family, which was next door to General Eisenhower's apartment. How amazing is that?

As children we perhaps did not understand the significance of this, but boy, we enjoyed playing in the woods nearby as well as playing 'ghosties' in the castle! Steeped in history, the Burns connection is strong at the castle and there is something quite magical about being there with the music and poetry resonating all around.

When I sing Burns songs, I am transported in my own mind back to Culzean and Ayrshire, and the landscape which influenced a man of the people. He was an extraordinary man who influenced and enriched 'The Enlightenment' in a way that I feel sure he was never truly aware.

Down by the burn, where scented birks
Wi dew are hangin clear, my jo,
I'll meet thee on the lea-rig,
My ain kind dearie, O!

The Lea-Rig

James Cosmo

Actor

Abraham Lincoln, when asked to write the foreword to an edition of the works of Robert Burns, his favourite poet, declined, stating that he felt unworthy to critique a talent as huge as Burns (I paraphrase). I would concur with that decision.

However, what I can tell you is that, on first reading Burns as a young man, it was his politics which had the most impact on me. Not that his more romantic work is not among the most beautiful ever written, but it was more that clear and incisive view of the injustices in his society that moved me. (Myself and a few million other folk I hasten to add.) The Burns of the boozy Supper has no interest for me, more it is the man who railed against the cant and hypocrisy of the day, who shared a vision with us of a just egalitarian world.

It is sad to reflect that many of the issues Burns addressed still poison our society. The vast majority of the land in Scotland is still in the hands of a tiny minority, denying living and breathing space to her rightful owners, the people of Scotland; we still give credence to a medieval and anachronistic system of honours, which, debased and corrupt, only serves to massage the hubris of some and the cynical dishonesty of others.

To me Robert Burns is not with the plump middle-classes, guzzling haggis and whisky once a year, he stands with the *Sans Culottes* at the Barricades, with the International Brigade and with the men in No Man's Land on Christmas Day 1914.

There was one song that Rab never wrote and I dearly wish he had reason to, that was a Scottish *La Marseillaise*.

Lay the proud usurpers low!
Tyrants fall in every foe!
Liberty's in every blow! –
Let us do, or die!

Scots Wha Hae

Paul Anderson

Fiddler and Fiddle Teacher

As a fiddle-playing farmer's son from the heart of Aberdeenshire, I've always felt a great deal of empathy for Robert Burns from the youngest age. I can easily relate to the back-breaking and unrelenting toil of working the land, and how you could love and hate it in equal measure; one day you can feel broken and drained, and the next, filled with inspiration and a joy too deep to explain.

The Scots fiddle tradition is an unbroken and living tradition which goes right back to a time before the arrival of the violin in Scotland around 1660. Prior to that, more primitive instruments like the 'rebec' and 'feythl' were played. By the late eighteenth century, the Golden Age of Scottish fiddle music had arrived and Scottish country dancing was enjoyed by all levels of society. At this time, the most famous fiddler and composer of the day was Niel Gow, from whom my own fiddle-playing lineage is descended.

Burns was also a fiddler, a fact which many people don't know, and although he was not renowned as a great player, I feel pretty sure that this ability to play helped him put his words to music. The melody for many of the now famous songs written by Burns were actually old Scots fiddle tunes; Burns knew a good tune when he heard it, and two of his favourites were 'The Rothiemurchus Rant' and 'Niel Gow's Lamentation for James Moray, Esq., of Abercarney.'

Niel Gow was, and still is, a legend, and during Burns tour of the Highlands in 1787 he undertook a considerable detour to visit Gow at his cottage at Inver near Dunkeld, where an afternoon of hospitality and music was enjoyed. How I wish I could have been there!

However, it's not Burns' fondness for the fiddle or his lifetime working on the land that touches me most; it's his use of the Scots language. Scots is my language, and it's the one in which I'm most comfortable, whether at home, in the pub or on the stage; it strikes to my core, and in a much more personal way than English ever can. It's the language of the fireside, the family, farmers and the land itself, and perhaps it's because the Scots language is virtually never heard in the media that the words of Burns mean that much more to me.

O, rattlin, roarin Willie,
    O, he held to the fair,
An for to sell his fiddle
    An buy some other ware;
But parting wi his fiddle,
    The saut tear blin't his e'e –
And rattlin, roarin Willie,
    Ye're welcome hame to me.

Rattlin, Roarin Willie

Jack Webster

Writer

The name of Robert Burns came early to my childhood in rural Aberdeenshire, when my grandmother told me I had his family blood in my veins. That came from her father Gavin Greig, distinguished poet, playwright, composer and folk-song collector, who could trace his connection to the farms of Brawlie-muir and Clochnahill near Stonehaven, where the Bard's father was brought up.

William Burnes was the one to head south, looking for work as a gardener, landing in Ayrshire and giving that county first claim on our national Bard. North-east folk have never got over the loss!

As five-year-olds at Maud School, we were asked by Miss Catto what we wanted to be when we grew up. She later told the staffroom of my reply: 'I want to be like Robbie Burns.' To her fellow-teachers she expressed the hope that I would not turn out to be too much like him! In Aberdeenshire, incidentally, we never called him Rabbie.

I was also telling her that I wanted to be a reporter – and never did I waver from the writing ambition. Influences can be subtle. Naturally, it was later before Burns' work seeped into the marrow of my being. Then you marvelled at the scope of his genius, produced in such a tragically short time.

I sought out the words of those who knew him, such as Professor Dugald Stewart, who said his manners were 'simple, manly and independent, but without anything that indicated forwardness, arrogance or vanity. He took his share in conversation but no more than belonged to him. Nothing was more remarkable than the fluency and precision and originality of his language when he spoke in company.' That tells you so much.

As a young reporter, covering the famous Peterhead Burns Supper in the early 1950s, I surveyed the elderly gathering and reflected that this tradition must surely die out. My generation would not be following on. Nearly fifty years later, I was back at that same supper, surveying another elderly gathering.

Yes, we had followed on right enough, I concluded – as I rose to propose *The Immortal Memory of Robert Burns*. I glanced at the full list of speakers who had led this toast, and found to my astonishment that the man who stood on the same spot exactly one hundred years earlier was none other than my own great-grandfather, Gavin Greig. Tradition is a remarkable force.

I had my years of extolling the Burns genius, from village halls to the Grand Ballroom of the Grosvenor House in Park Lane, taking the message to a thousand London bankers, who were as attentive an audience as I had known. For Robert Burns strikes a universal chord, articulating everything from 'Man's inhumanity to man' right through to 'The best laid schemes o' mice and men/Gang aft agley'.

His spirit gives Scots people a focal point for their Scottishness, but within the context of a much wider world.

Brawlinmuir, Glenbervie, Kincardineshire

where James Burness, the poet's great-grandfather, was a tenant farmer. He died here on 23 January 1743 and is buried at Glenbervie Churchyard. Robert Burns' grandfather, also Robert, was born at Brawlinmuir in 1686.

Peter Westwood

Editor of *The Burns Chronicle*

It is not the individual songs and poems of Robert Burns that have made an impression on my life, although many of them have, but his works in general through my study of his letters to friends and associates. For his works span the whole spectrum of human experience.

Hardly a week passes without my thoughts turning to aspects of his genius – for even in today's troubled world, his thoughts on life and the brotherhood of man are still very relevant – if only the world would listen.

Burns speaks in a language we can understand; part of his genius lies in his ability to distil great thoughts into simple stanzas. He makes me proud and patriotic, he makes me ashamed of man's inhumanity to man, he shows me the beauties of nature, and he opens my eyes to the pathos of the human situation – for example in these lines from 'To a Mouse' on turning her up from her nest:

> Still thou art blest, compar'd wi' me!
> The present only toucheth thee:
> But och! I backward cast my e'e,
>   On prospects drear!
> An forward, tho I canna see,
>   I guess an fear!'

His youngest son, James Glencairn Burns, writing to his mother from India in 1813, told her: 'I have been reading his works very carefully lately, and really like his letters better than the poetry . . . what would I give to have a part of his abilities?'

The most famous of all Americans, President Abraham Lincoln, when asked to propose a toast to Burns, replied: 'I cannot frame a toast to Burns, I can say nothing of his generous heart, and transcending genius. Thinking of what he has said, I cannot say anything which seems worth saying.'

Within the poet's works are words or verses suitable for almost any occasion – happy or sad. I regularly consult a collection of quotations by him which cover 365 days of the year. In my role as editor of *The Burns Chronicle* I am often asked for words or verses suitable for, as an example, someone who has passed away:

> An honest man here lies at rest,
> As e'er God with his image blest:
> The friend of man, the friend of truth,
> The friend of age, and guide of youth:
> Few hearts like his – with virtue warm'd,
> Few heads with knowledge so inform'd:
> If there's another world, he lives in bliss;
> If there is none, he made the best of this.

Or words to go with a gift —

> O, could I give thee India's wealth,
> As I this trifle send!
> Because thy joy in both would be
> To share them with a friend!

I am about to celebrate our Golden Wedding, and my wife says it seems 30 of those years have been shared with Robert Burns!

Kincardineshire
fatherland of Robert Burns

James Grant

Musician and Songwriter

When I went to Primary School in the 1970s, besides the paucity in teaching of Scottish history or culture in general, there seemed to be a purge on the Scots dialect. We were constantly being corrected for our pronunciation, and told off or given the strap for sounding like our parents. Somehow, Robert Burns seemed to slip through the net, I suppose it would have been overkill to have omitted him.

I remember reading *Tam o' Shanter* and 'To a Mouse' but, to be honest, perhaps as a consequence of this eradication/anglicization, I found them quaint and unappealing. Down in Ayrshire, there'd be signs of the raffish geezer with the big sideburns directing us to various artefacts of the man, but, at the time, it all felt outmoded.

I erroneously lumped him in with the tartan and shortbread image of Scotland that was presented to us as entertainment on television; part of something we were desperate (with good reason) to leave behind.

Although I read voraciously (I've always been a bit paranoid about my lack of formal education and tried to compensate for it this way), I never went back to Burns. Childhood prejudices are often the hardest to break.

It didn't really strike me what I'd been missing until about ten years ago, when I started working with Karen Matheson and Donald Shaw from the band Capercaillie. I had written a couple of songs for Karen's first solo album, 'The Dreaming Sea', and they invited me to a concert they were playing before we started working together.

It was then I heard Karen's peerless version of 'Ae Fond Kiss'. I remember being utterly transfixed; there was an elemental, visceral quality to the words. I was struck by phrases like, 'and then we sever', 'warring sighs and groans I'll wage thee'. The song encompassed a burning intensity and passion, undiminished by time. It was, in essence, a great song beautifully sung which, for me, is what it's all about.

It might sound strange, but those three minutes re-opened the works of Robert Burns to me, and instead of being embarrassed by those words, I am in thrall to them. He has been depicted, rightly so, as our national bard and a true man of the people, a figurehead for our democratic spirit.

He is also, perhaps, our greatest songwriter.

Had I a cave on some wild distant shore,
Where the winds howl to the wave's dashing roar,
There would I weep my woes,
There seek my lost repose.

Had I a Cave

David Sibbald

Burns Presenter and Writer

Robert Burns was one of the most charismatic people ever to have walked on this earth. Yet even today, 250 years after his birth, he is misunderstood by many.

Robert Burns was a complex individual. We can look at different aspects of his character almost as if we were looking at the facets of a diamond. Each facet has a clarity, a depth and a brilliance.

Firstly there is Burns the poet.

It was his poems which initially assured him of a worldwide stage. Poems that are full of fun. Poems that champion the poor and oppressed. Satires against the hypocrisy and cant of the Calvinistic church. Philosophies and observations of life and its people. His concern for human rights and his love of friendship. His poems can pierce your soul.

Burns the songwriter.

It was into his songs that Burns' consummate literary craftsmanship breathed a rejuvenating life and spirit, and a consistently all-pervading honesty and sincerity. Burns rescued over 370 songs from obscurity and neglect.

Burns the letter writer.

His correspondents included the Prime Minister, clergymen, doctors, lawyers and the cream of literary society of his day. He immersed himself in the affairs of the time, political and social, writing to John Francis Erskine, the 27th Earl of Mar as follows:

'Does any man tell me, that my feeble efforts can be of no service; that it does not belong to my humble station to meddle with the concerns of a People? – I tell him, that it is on such individuals as I, that for the hand of support and the eye of intelligence, a Nation has to rest.'

At that time only the wealthy had a vote, and yet Burns, one of the greatest intellects to walk the world's stage, who mingled at ease in conversation with the aristocracy, had no vote.

Burns the patriot and politician.

Robert Burns was quintessentially Scottish. Almost everything he did was political. His writing of songs was done for no remuneration. He knew that a nation without song had no soul. He knew that a nation without song would lose its identity. He kept alive the idea that there was such a thing as a Scottish nation. He helped to keep our belief in ourselves breathing through a long, long hibernation. The truth is that Scotland would have a different identity, if it had not been for Robert Burns.

Burns was universal and a humanitarian.

He was able to take everyday events, as in 'To a Mouse', for example, and turn them into universal truths. His poetry speaks of breaking down international barriers, of championing human rights, and standing up and being a voice for oppressed people throughout the world.

If 'Auld Lang Syne' is the world's national anthem, then 'A Man's a Man' is the *Marsellaise* to humanity.

Personally, I believe that in Burns' works you will find a lifetime of pleasure, hope, inspiration and courage. He stands for friendship above all, but encompasses honesty, integrity and truth.

He helps you to know yourself.

While Summer, with a matron grace,
Retreats to Dryburgh's cooling shade,
Yet oft, delighted, stops to trace
The progress of the spikey blade.

Address to the Shade of Thomson

Jennifer Wilson

Director of Burnsong

It's hard not to be touched by Robert Burns, when you live a few miles from Ellisland, marginally more from Dumfries (where his Theatre Royal still provides entertainment), and have a heart like melting butter. Not to mention being married to an Ayr-born school prize-winning reader of *Tam o' Shanter*. Robert Burns had reached me not simply through the spoken poems (I'm English), but also the letters, which are to be relished, and the songs which I now manage to sing along to. I live in his landscape.

Aside from the personal, Robert Burns has had a steady presence in my working life in Scotland, since I arrived 30 years ago. In my work at the Crawford Centre at the University of St Andrews, images of him featured in Murray and Barbara Grigor's 1981 iconic 'Scotch Myths' exhibition – postcards, posters and music contributed to this wry and penetrating look at Scots and Scottishness which found its way to the Edinburgh Festival the same year.

At Dumfries and Galloway Arts Association, Burns has been a constant companion – not as a traditional icon, but as a touchstone for new and contemporary activities. Involvement in the 1996 celebrations came via a community lantern event with 10,000 participants and a fiery portrait in Dumfries town centre. A Robert Burns Creative Writing Fellowship continues, focusing on contemporary Scots writing, and in 2003, Burnsong itself was born.

It arose from a casual discussion as to what, in contemporary terms, Robert Burns might be today? Poet, yes, but for our times, a songwriter – so the project that supports songwriting and celebrates new and emergent songwriters was born. A collective brainstorm confirmed the important things about Robert Burns in the 21st century – his humanity, egalitarianism, interest in nature, affections and humour, new and collected songs, and the very contemporary aspect of Scotland's sense of its importance in the world.

Burnsong has grown – it has strands to involve individuals and communities. The Burns and Rivers education project, with an excellent pack and strong connections with environmental issues; the Gathering of new songs via an open invitation to submit, and the presentation of these songs at the Big Gig, and live events; the creation of the innovative and effective Songhouse concept, where eight established songwriters retreat for a week, and through new collaborations, create new songs, later showcased on tour, or at festivals.

Burnsong seeks the new, and supports those who create it, inviting everyone to 'discover the song inside' and to share their work with others, in the spirit of Burns himself. Over two and a half thousand people have been directly involved so far – in schools, submitting songs, attending gigs – and the Songhouse concept has been widely welcomed, and enjoyed, by a rich mix of Scotland's songwriters. Midge Ure's acceptance of the role of the first Patron is welcomed as proof that Burnsong has found not only an important role, but the right path to support songs, and the sharing of songs, in Scotland and around the world.

I hope that Robert Burns would approve – I think he would, and if he were here, I'd hope he might chair the selection panel – unless he preferred to send us his songs, of course.

Adown winding Nith I did wander,
To mark the sweet flowers as they spring.
Adown winding Nith I did wander,
Of Phillis to muse and to sing.

Adown Winding Nith

Jimmie Macgregor

Writer, Broadcaster and Musician

He is still with us. He still affects us. We are awed by the colossal output of his short life and amazed by the giant talent and all-embracing humanity.

In his thirties, he was already complaining of the rapidly deteriorating physical condition which was to take him so soon.

> But och! I backward cast my e'e,
> On prospects drear!
> An forward, tho I canna see,
> I guess an fear!

Everyone is acquainted with the comedian who is dull and withdrawn when not performing, and the actor who is inarticulate when separated from the script. This was not Burns. Despite his health problems and suffering the trials of a man of genius born as a peasant in a class-ridden society, people who met him were invariably struck by his vigour, his brilliance in conversation and the sheer life force which emanated from him.

In Sir Walter Scott's famous description of the poet, he says, 'The eye alone, I think, indicated the poetical character and temperament. It was large and of a dark cast, and glowed (I say literally glowed) when he spoke with feeling or interest. I never saw such an eye in a human head.' (The actor, playwright and musician David Anderson developed the rather whimsical notion that Scott's comment could have led to the belief that Burns had only one eye.)

Theories are many as to Robert Burns' physical appearance, and again, Scott is helpful. 'I think his countenance was more massive than it looks in any of the portraits.' There has certainly been much suspicion of the glamorised, even effeminate representations by Skirving and Nasmith, and there are accounts of the poet which come closer to the chunky, slightly stooped physique we would expect of a man used to physical labour.

He is also said to have had what Americans describe as an over-bite, and that characteristic is evident in the 1787 silhouette by Meir. Burns himself claimed this as his most accurate likeness. Most people appear to be quite happy to believe that he looked like actor John Cairney, as is John Cairney, I should imagine. All the evidence indicates that Burns was never as good looking as John was, and still is.

Many actors have played Burns. Tom Wright's first choice for the lead in his definitive play 'There Was a Man' was Maurice Roeves, and Victor Carin played the part before Cairney. Nevertheless, John Cairney has put his indelible stamp on the character, and has since become a recognised authority on the poet's life and work, picking up a hard won PhD in the process.

The truth is that we shall never know exactly what the poet looked like. More importantly, we have access to the wonderful insight, lyricism and compassion of one of the truly great human beings.

Ye burnies, wimplin down your glens,
Wi toddlin din,
Or foaming, strang, wi hasty stens,
Frae lin to lin!

Elegy on Captain Matthew Henderson

Professor David W. Purdie

Writer and Broadcaster

Born and bred at Prestwick in Ayrshire just a few miles from the cottage which bears his name, I have simply had Burns as a companion since childhood. I learned much from my father, a fine Immortal Memorist, while Ayr Academy's masters made sure that we young scholars absorbed the biography of the man alongside the study of his poems and songs.

When I was appointed to a Chair at the university I received a stern letter from home directing me never, ever, to forget 'Epistle to Davie' v.5. It's the famous passage which runs 'It's no in titles, nor in rank…' and ends '…The heart aye's the part, aye,/ That makes us right or wrang.' And that surely is the essence of the poet's moral stance, his criterion of the true worth of a man. It is determined, says Burns, not by inherited wealth or position in society, not in the magnitude of his intellect, or any title before his name. It lies, rather, in the nature of his heart, and the space therein which he reserves for the weal and the welfare of his fellow men.

Much later I came across an entry in Walter Scott's *Journal* which will chime with many of you who read this book and with many of us who contributed to it. He wrote 'Long life to thy fame and peace to thy soul, Rob Burns. When I want to express any sentiment strongly, I find the phrase in Shakespeare – or in thee.'

No wonder our emigrants placed the works of Burns in the family kist when they packed to go on their long journeys to the St Lawrence, to the Cape of Storms or over the wild southern ocean to Australia and New Zealand. It was not just because he spoke and sang to them in the accents of home. It was for companionship. It was because he always has something to say, to the struggling farmer, to the uncertain lover, to the young soldier facing his first action. And the refrain, in a score of poems and songs, is: courage, brother, do not falter – and *never* despair. And that is what he said to me.

And so, over the years, at Suppers for his memory, I have tried to repay my companion for his company. First in plain prose, and now with images from the national archive and with the singing of Sheena Wellington or Aileen Carr, I try to retell the great story. The story of how a child born in a two-roomed Ayrshire cottage became one of the finest lyric poets and songwriters ever to lift a pen and, incidentally, a fine companion for my long journey – and yours.

What tho, like commoners of air,
We wander out, we know not where,
    But either house or hal'?
Yet Nature's charms, the hills and woods,
The sweeping vales, and foaming floods,
    Are free alike to all.

Epistle to Davie, a Brother Poet

Malky McCormick

Caricaturist

Being born in Glasgow and having lived in Ayrshire for the past 36 years, I'm a proud Weegie interlouper and admirer of Robert Burns.

Although he enjoyed being one of the streetwise boys, sittin' bousin' at the nappy, gettin' fou 'n' unco happy, Burns was a gentle romantic. I believe his love for all around him and the beautiful Ayrshire countryside proved the inspiration for his work.

My own feeling for the outdoors has taken me to locations close to Burns – the West Highlands, the Galloway Hills, Dumfries and my own favourite spot that pays tribute to him – the Burns Cairn overlooking Afton Water at Laight Farm. This idyllic wee burn has its source on the slopes of Alwhat Hill, it flows through Glen Afton and joins the River Nith at New Cumnock. When I hill walk this area, his song is in my mind.

The River Nith, of course, wanders south through Dumfries on its way to the Solway Firth. Dumfries is a beautiful town for any enthusiast to visit. Around every corner, there appears to be a landmark frequented by him. Recently a great Doonhamer pal of mine, Alex Inman, whom I met while walking the Inca Trail in Peru, showed me round the Burns House, the Mausoleum, the Globe and Hole in the Wall pubs and left me thinking, 'Whaur's yir Machu Pichu noo?'

All the towns associated with Burns are special, but times in Ayr, the *Tam o' Shanter* parody runs through my mind –

> Auld Ayr, where ne'er a town surpasses,
> For pullin' tails aff horses' asses.

(This is a reference to Tam's mare Meg crossing Alloway Brig!)

Then there are Tarbolton, Kirkoswald, Maybole and Kilmarnock with its fine Sandy Stoddart statue at the cross. This monument of Robert Burns and his printer commemorates the publication of the first edition of his work.

Mauchline is special for me. As part of the 'Burns an' A' That' annual festival, Mauchline holds 'The Holy Fair' – a great free event. Parades, locals in period costume, stalls and a music stage make it a great day. Musicians such as Donnie Munro, Gaberlunzie and Michael Marra have taken the place by storm. A real Rave for Rab! I've been a guest for several years to do lightning caricatures of the townsfolk – 'Drawing a Big Crowd'. Eventually, the entire town adjourns to Poosie Nancy's for a collective 'Wattin' of the Whistle'. *Slainte*!

I have taken part in many Burns Suppers in places at home and around the world, e.g. from my local pub, the Kings Arms in Fenwick, to the Crowne Plaza Hotel in Kuwait City. At these events, part of my 'act' is to draw quick 'flip chart cartoons' to illustrate the talk. At the Kuwait supper, myself and my 6ft 1in pal Colin Howie performed 'The Twa Dogs' (Little and Large). This presentation was enjoyed immensely by the participants, though largely ignored by the audience!

I will always be grateful to Robert Burns for enabling me to travel the world. In Russia, of course, he is an icon and I have personally experienced the friendship and camaraderie there.

Back home to Ayrshire, where a couple of years ago, at our local Burns Supper, I proposed 'The Toast to the Lassies' and my wife Ann responded with a clever and pointed 'Reply from the Lassies' – Beware o' Bonnie Ann!

Finally, I would like to acknowledge Robert Burns and his influence on my work and me by reproducing his poem 'To an Artist':

> Dear ——, I'll gie ye some advice,
>   You'll tak it no uncivil:
> You shouldna paint at angels, man,
>   But try to paint the Devil.
>
> To paint an angel's kittle wark,
>   Wi' Nick there's little danger:
> You'll easy draw a lang-kent face,
>   But no sae weel a stranger.

Garvock Tap, near Laurencekirk, Kincardineshire
where William and Robert Burnes, the poet's father and uncle, parted company as young men in 1748 to seek better fortune in the south. They never saw each other again.

Richard Gowring

Great-Great-Great-Grandson of Robert Burns

I cannot remember exactly how old I was when it first dawned on me that I was related to the greatest Scottish poet of all time. I can remember, however, the bookcase on the Sixth Form wall of my Prep School in Eastbourne, where there were two volumes of the *Complete Works of Robert Burns*.

I remember, on one occasion, taking down one of the volumes and being totally dismayed because I could not understand a single word of the great works within. Here were the writings of my great-great-great grandfather, but what he was saying was incomprehensible to me!

Undaunted by my ignorance, I decided to impress the teacher in charge of afternoon 'prep'. I took the volume up to him and asked him to explain the meaning of one of the verses to me. I told him – in passing – that Robert Burns was my great-great-great grandfather. This announcement was met with complete indifference, and he told me not to be silly and to go and sit down again; so much for my quest for stardom and fame!

I have to admit that, after leaving school and for the next 30 years or so, the wonders of my forebear's great writings took second place to my career in the Royal Air Force and bringing up a family. It was the organiser of the World Federation of Burns Clubs event in Sheffield in the early 1990s who changed all that. He telephoned me to ask if, by any chance, I knew the whereabouts of 2 silver candlesticks, and a candle-snuffer and tray, which were (in 1821) 'The GIFT of a few SCOTS in SHEFFIELD to the Widow of Burns'. I was able to tell him that I knew exactly where they were, and, arising out of this, I was kindly invited to attend the dinner in Sheffield that concluded the event – accompanied of course by the famous silverware.

That dinner in Sheffield transformed my outlook on the works of my famous forebear. Until that occasion, I had no idea of the extent of the reverence in which he is held throughout the world, an appreciation that was reinforced when I was subsequently involved in the bi-centenary events commemorating his death in 1996.

To this day, I remain humbled by the awe in which I was regarded simply because of who I was (by accident of birth) rather than for anything I had done. I can think of no other poet or author who commands such widespread acclaim and devotion. In modern parlance, no doubt, he would have been regarded by most Scots at the time as 'the People's Poet'.

As a direct descendant, it is impossible for me not to be touched by the writings of this great man. But, unlike those early days of complete incomprehension of his works, I can at least now show some understanding and appreciation of the inspiring words within them. But, oh for a small measure of the man's great genius!

When lyart leaves bestrow the yird,
Or, wavering like the bauckie-bird,
 Bedim cauld Boreas' blast;
When hailstanes drive wi bitter skyte,
And infant frosts begin to bite,
 In hoary cranreuch drest…

The Jolly Beggars – A Cantata

Dame Evelyn Glennie

Percussionist

Hogmanays are not what they used to be! As far back as I can remember, the farmhouse roof nearly lifted off with our yearly exuberant rendition of 'Auld Lang Syne' – my introduction to Rabbie Burns, as we referred to him.

I have since lost count of the number of times I have joined hands with a multitude of folks from around the globe, singing and swaggering to what must arguably be the most recognisable melody and lyrics ever to be written. It's also interesting to observe the subtlety in rhythmical interpretation of this song; the 'Scots Snap' generally and understandably being more prevalent in Scotland than in other territories, and one never fails to experience the sheer passion that people from all over feel towards this big little gem.

My desire to learn the Great Highland Bagpipes was partly ignited by the wish to participate in a Burns Night as the piper to accompany the entrance and cutting of the haggis. We are all aware of the popularity of Burns Suppers throughout the world, which I must say would be an excellent event to replicate in schools to help ignite that spark of curiosity in our young people about the magnitude of Robert Burns and his work. I have spent hours trying to perfect the melody of 'A Man's a Man for A' That' on my pipes – not easy, but thoroughly rewarding (my neighbours may have another opinion!).

It is all too easy to forget that Burns died whilst still a young man; the statues placed throughout the world and the universal cult-following belie the fact that his life was short, and one can only wonder how different things might be if extra years were at his disposal. This, in itself, is of influence, knowing that if one can find the key to what really makes each of us light up, we too can make a difference.

As I travel throughout the world, armed with my north-east brogue, I'm amazed to see how many people launch into Burns prose or song as a tribute to meeting a genuine Scot! The ice is broken as the words 'Robert Burns' are uttered, and we know that relations are off to a healthy start. As a Doric speaker myself, I know the importance of reading, writing and speaking a dialect to keep it alive, and the fascination it can have for others. The accessibility of Burns' writing is shown by his awareness in acknowledging and respecting his local dialect, but yet making it accessible to a wider audience. As we live in what is becoming a more flat world, it is even more important to retain and share the richness of our local language.

I cannot imagine any youngster leaving school not being familiar with at least the name Robert Burns. Thanks to technology, if not an old fashioned Hogmanay, the legacy of Burns continues to burn brightly.

There's not a bonie flower that springs
By fountain, shaw, or green,
There's not a bonie bird that sings,
But minds me o my Jean

Of A' the Airts

HE Dr Lindiwe Mabuza

High Commissioner of the Republic of South Africa to the United Kingdom

Before I came across any poetry written in a foreign language, I had already started memorising some Zulu poems. Yes, some things we had to learn by rote. To this day, I can still recite some extracts from the great epics capturing the lifetimes or events around our kings: Shaka Zulu, Dingane Zulu or Mpande Zulu, all written by R.R. Dlomo.

We learned quite early that the beauty of poetry, its lasting appeal, was its musicality, the colours it paints, the scents, smells, odours it evokes and the lessons it teaches. Didactic, it often helped the reader to discern the good from the bad, the acceptable from the unacceptable.

When I came across poetry written in the English language, I was in a Catholic Girls' High School for blacks only, St Lewis Bertrand, Newcastle. Our school was situated in a scenic edge of Lennoxton, with Incandu River meandering around and beyond and far away from the school's huge vegetable garden. The wide-open field across the river swept across for miles till it was stopped by the majestic Ukhahlamba Mountains, always covered with snow at the top all winter long.

My school was run by white Dominican nuns: Irish, German and South African. About a mile from our school was another Catholic Girls' High School, St Dominic, for whites only, also run by Dominican nuns. Though we were in racially separated schools, we sat for the same provincial examinations at the end of the year and therefore had the same syllabus and books. One day our Principal, Sister Rieti, and our English literature teacher, Sister Maelisa, decided to take our class for a visit to our sister school. We were immediately struck by the differences between this school and ours. They had a library, whereas we didn't; they had a laboratory and we had to memorise how experiments were carried out. Their dining tables had tablecloths, ours didn't. Everything was superior, which of course suggested they were inherently superior as apartheid suggested to us. Their superiority was materially engineered and therefore guaranteed. But our school always scored higher results in the same tests than the white girls' school.

This is the context and time we come across Robert Burns' poem: 'A Man's a Man for A' That'. Here was a white man in a different country, Scotland, telling us about discrimination in society based, not on colour, but on arbitrary socio-economic reasons: rank or class, or social status. He had an instant appeal when he reminded his world that 'rank is but the guinea's stamp'; pomp and circumstance, a 'tinsel show'. If clothes did not make a man or woman, how then, we would argue in class, can colour define the character, content, qualities and the essence of anyone. If honesty and integrity should be held in higher esteem than all the superficial symbols of refinement, what makes white people think they are more important than our parents? The poem had resonance and immediate relevance for us.

Burns was saying to us that notwithstanding the circumstances of your birth and the prescriptions society imposes, you can actually be superior to those who pronounce you inferior. Self worth, self confidence and an independent mind seemed infinitely more crucial, a *sine qua non* in navigating through life.

Dost ask me, why I send thee here,
The firstling of the infant year?
Dost ask me, what this primrose shews,
Bepearled thus with morning dews?

  I must whisper to thy ears,
  The sweets of love are wash'd with tears.

The Primrose

In Burns' poetry we found some commonality but also a rich vocabulary in the names of flowers, like the primrose, the hawthorns and white daisies, and new birds with Scottish names. The world away from ours was perhaps different mainly, or perhaps only, in name. Exposure to the beauty of the Scottish environment made us more aware of our own landscapes, our flora and fauna, and it engendered love and appreciation of our own environmental beauty.

We found the 'Lament of Mary, Queen of Scots' especially poignant. Here, the pastoral beauty of Scotland, nature's grandeur, the azure skies, the sweet music of its birds is shattered by the cruel reality that the Queen of Scottish people 'lies in prison'. The parallel to our situation was dramatic and inescapable. In centuries past, our own royalty had been sent off to St Helena Island or Robben Island by white rulers. Our fathers, uncles, brothers and any black male was likely to end up in jail because of the most hated and notorious pass laws, the badge of slavery. In later years, of course, our own leaders like Nelson Mandela, Walter Sisulu, Govan Mbeki, Dorothy Nyembe and countless others would end up spending over two decades in prison incarcerated by impostors who usurped power.

In Queen Mary's bitter acrimony towards 'Thou false woman, my sister and my foe' we found a betrayal and treachery similar to that of King Dingane Zulu who assassinated his own brother, King Shaka Zulu.

Yet in our history books, the white authors wrote of our kings in the most derogatory and insulting manner, characterizing them as 'primitive bloodthirsty warmongers.' In Queen Mary's lament we discovered that Queen Elizabeth I of England had dethroned and imprisoned Queen Mary and thus was responsible for her death. It became evident to us through literature that Africans did not have a monopoly on bad deeds. It was clear that white people had a propensity for the most gross crimes.

When, around this same period, we learnt in our religion class of the Reformation and Henry VIII and his beheaded wives, it appeared to us that white people were infinitely more superior in evil deeds. Literature for us was alive with history documenting dastardly behaviour, even deep inside royal households!

The very first love poem written in English I came across was Burns' 'My Luve's like a Red, Red Rose'. As we analysed the poem we were being introduced to various figures of speech in the English language: metaphor, simile, onomatopoeia, oxymoron etc. But this declaration of love did not only teach us that nature is the best subject for discerning artists. It also taught us that observing nature and its ever-changing properties enriches poetic expression. The fine delicacy and scent of the rich, red rose, aligned to the sweetness of music, conjured up the power of love to make the impossible possible.

> And I will luve thee still, my dear,
> Till a' the seas gang dry…
> And the rocks melt wi' the sun.

But my sentimentality was dealt a blow one day when spontaneously one of my classmates asked our teacher how she should respond if ever called 'My red, red rose' by a boyfriend in future. This was almost sacrilege. We were never supposed to think about, let alone talk to nuns of boyfriends. This was one cardinal unwritten rule. Some girls started giggling, but the one who asked the question was poker-faced.

'Yes! Yes! I mean, no! No!' said the white teacher, turning beet-red. 'You do not blush, you see,' she explained! There was pandemonium and a chorus: 'Sister, you are blushing! Sister, you are blushing!' – the chant ricocheted around the room. When calm returned, another student explained to the nun, who was still rosy in the face, 'Maybe it's good not to blush; then the world does not see our joys and pains. Our dark skin hides our blushing.' Actually, I don't think any of us were compared to a rose! Ever!

However, I liked this poem so much that I secretly put it into music so that I would always remember the lyrics. I have never shared my melody with anyone else in the world, but I can remember the song still to this day. This is how much the Bard influenced my development as a teenager 'ten thousand miles away' from his environment and theatre of activities.

Decades later, in 1973 when I was myself writing poetry and teaching literature, this very poem of Burns provided one of the images in a poem I wrote protesting at the buying of South African diamonds:

Agape: Tomorrow

When they seal love
With smiling clusters of diamond
They never tell about the dark depths looming behind

When they say love
Is like a red red rose
Some never tell about the green thorns guarding the petals

Nor can they who remember
Fully relish the honeycomb
When the thumb swells blue from all the stings

But in the free and obedient hive of our growing love
Worker bees honour
The rose
Erect... the brilliance
Of the future
Partaking of today's dark thorns.

It was not until 2002 that I discovered the most remarkable aspect of Burns, his opposition to slavery in a poem called 'The Slave's Lament'. We were preparing to have a Burns Night at South Africa House in London. The reason for this was that during the struggle against apartheid, some of the Scottish friends of the African National Congress (ANC) organised Burns Night events in order to raise funds for the ANC. On one of these occasions, Chris Hani was the guest of honour. My own passion for literature and a little knowledge of Burns plus a sense of gratitude to the Scottish people who participated so concretely in our liberation struggle made us want to do something in memory of Robert Burns and in celebration of Scottish-South African solidarity.

Brian Filling, the former President of the Scottish Anti-Apartheid movement and now President of Scottish ACTSA sent me 'The Slave's Lament' to present as part of the program. I was completely overwhelmed by some emotional turmoil on reading this poem. Here was Burns, a white man, jumping out of his privileged white world and white skin to figuratively and emotionally enter the body, mind, soul and sensibilities of an African slave 'torn from that lovely shore' of Senegal.

The word 'torn' cut deep inside the womb. That tearing works on several levels – the physical separation, being geographically uprooted from one's country; alienation from all that is familiar and normal culture... sights... kingship... sounds... laughter... loss of one's sense of being and identity... loss of orientation and point of reference; an imposed new identity; chains cutting into the flesh; the whip; the sizzling of the branding iron; the meticulously orchestrated 'breaking' of who you are, because all fundamental elements that define the Africans' humaneness must rupture. The anguish was total. Certainly this poem put Robert Burns in the abolitionist camp with great authors like Mark Twain and William Wordsworth, to name two more.

Whenever I have presented the poem to an audience, there has been an amazing reaction. But for me the greatest honour was presenting it in Glasgow at the Robert Burns Supper of 25th January 2004, hosted by the Lord Provost, Councillor Liz Cameron, in the presence of the Lord Provost of Edinburgh, Councillor Lesley Hinds, and the 1000 guests. There was a thunderous applause at the end of the presentation. I was very grateful to have the opportunity to give back to the Scottish audience my own inheritance from their native son, Robert Burns.

In this brief exposé of my encounter with Robert Burns, I have deliberately excluded some unsavoury aspects of Robert Burns' life. These come out in his many poems dedicated to many women; the womanising side of Burns, which bedevils pages of his complete works. The poems I have commented on will always remain seminal reference points for my understanding and appreciation of this great poet. He was a great outsider who entered our young lives and made it fun to look through and poke at the veneer of white skin and have our day laughing at their wrong and distorted assumptions and perceptions of us. Like him and with him, we craved to be most human.

And there's a hand my trusty fiere,
And gie's a hand o thine,
And we'll tak a right guid-willie waught,
For auld lang syne.

Auld Lang Syne

A Brief Biography of Robert Burns

Robert Burns, Scotland's international poet, was born in a small thatched cottage in Alloway, Ayrshire, on 25 January, 1759.

His father, William Burnes, was an agricultural worker from the county of Kincardineshire in the north-east of Scotland. Having travelled to Ayrshire, via Edinburgh, to a better life than the Mearns could offer him, William met and married Agnes Brown from the parish of Kirkoswald. They had seven children, Robert being the eldest.

When Robert was seven years of age, his father took over the tenancy of Mount Oliphant Farm, not far from the village of Alloway. From an early age, Robert had to work on the farm – rain wind or shine – for hours at a time.

In between his work on the farm, from the ages of six to sixteen, Robert received several spells of schooling under the tutelage of James Murdoch. His father held education in very high regard, and did everything he could to provide Robert with as extensive an education as his tiny income would allow. While at Mount Oliphant, Robert wrote his first poem in praise of a Nellie Kilpatrick, entitled "Handsome Nell". They were both fourteen and she was paired with Robert at the harvest.

After eleven years of trying to make a meagre living from the land, William Burnes gave up his tenancy and moved his family to Lochlie Farm, not far from Tarbolton. Although the work was still extremely hard, Robert enjoyed a full social life in the nearby village, forming the Bachelors' Club with friends in 1780, and getting to know the young ladies of the parish.

From Lochlie, Robert travelled to Irvine for eight months to learn the trade of dressing flax, but he disliked the work and his employer, spending most of the period feeling miserable and dispirited.

On his return to Lochlie, his father became involved in a legal dispute with his landlord, and had all his possessions sequestrated. Although the legal case was settled in his father's favour, it had a very detrimental effect on his health and he died in 1784.

In less than a month, the family moved to the farm of Mossgiel near Mauchline, with Robert and his brother Gilbert taking over the lease. Although the land was unforgiving, the brothers worked hard to sustain the family.

Despite their toil, the crops at Mossgiel failed in the early part of their tenancy, and the brothers struggled to make anything of the poor crops they grew thereafter. Robert became very downhearted and took solace in the writing of poems. Before long, his output became prolific, and occupied much of his time away from the fields. While at Mossgiel, Robert changed the spelling of the family name from Burnes to Burns.

In Mauchline, Burns began a relationship with Jean Armour and with Highland Mary (Mary Campbell), both of whom became subjects of his poetry. When Jean became pregnant, Robert had a marriage affirmation document drawn up, signed by them both. This was a valid procedure in old Scots law, but Jean Armour's father refused to recognise Burns as his son-in-law, bringing their relationship to a temporary close.

As a result of Jean Armour's father's antipathy towards him and the poor opportunities in farming, Robert decided to relocate to the West Indies. At the same time, and partly to help finance the trip, he published *Poems, Chiefly in the Scottish Dialect*, now famously known as "The Kilmarnock Edition", in 1786. It was an instant success, so much so that he gave up all plans to emigrate to Jamaica.

The subject matter of his poetry resonated with people from all walks of life and from all social classes. The book contained verses dealing with love, humour, repression, compassion and all aspects of the human condition. As a result of the publication, Burns visited Edinburgh and toured extensively throughout Scotland, including the land of his fathers in Kincardineshire.

Before long he was being fêted by Edinburgh Society. An enlarged edition of his poems, "The Edinburgh Edition" was published in 1787 by William Creech.

Early in 1788, the poet returned to Mossgiel. Following Jean Armour's abandonment by her parents for becoming pregnant, Robert and Jean married and began a new life in Mauchline.

Several months later, Robert took over the tenancy of Ellisland Farm near Dumfries. He went on ahead to set up the farm, leaving Jean in Mauchline, but she soon joined him.

Repeating the pattern experienced by his father of constantly having to work difficult and infertile land, Burns decided to take up a position as an Exciseman in addition to his farm work. Notwithstanding this double labour, he still managed to produce an enormous amount of letters and poetry.

Gradually, as a result of a lifetime of hard effort on the land, Robert's health began to deteriorate to the point that he decided to give up the tenancy of Ellisland. He moved with Jean and his growing family into Dumfries to continue working with the Excise.

In 1793, the Burns family moved to Mill Vennel in Dumfries, now 24 Burns Street. The second Edinburgh Edition of his poems was published by William Creech, this one including Tam o' Shanter, which Burns had written at Ellisland.

Throughout 1795, he became gravely ill with rheumatic fever. He continued to work until June 1796, but his health was failing rapidly. He died in Dumfries on 21 July 1796, aged only 37.

Crowds lined the streets at his funeral. As the cortège made its way to the churchyard, Jean gave birth to their son, Maxwell.

The poet's remains, along with those of his wife Jean, are buried in the Burns Mausoleum at St Michael's Churchyard in Dumfries.

Acknowledgements

In the course of researching and producing *Touched by Robert Burns*, I've received assistance from a variety of sources. Primarily, my thanks go to all the contributors, who have embraced the idea of the book with commitment and enthusiasm.

I would particularly like to acknowledge the contribution of Raeburn, Christie, Clark and Wallace (Solicitors) of Aberdeen and my good friend Keith Allan for sponsorship of travel and accommodation; Eddie Cairns and Neil Gove (*www.neilgove.co.uk*) for computer, digital camera and software support; Paul Back of Galashiels (*www.garrionstudio.com*) for permission to use his wonderful sculpted bust for the cover image; Niall and Jacqueline Irvine of Perspectives (*www.perspectivesnet.com*) for, once again, providing me with excellent scans and creative support; the students of Aberdeen University and Fiona Bain for their assistance in setting up and making themselves available for the graduation image; my daughter Lynsey and her friend Ross Davidson for modelling for the 'Ae Fond Kiss' image; John Valentine, Geordie Murison and Jim Taylor; Wilhelm Hermanns of the Heugh Hotel in Stonehaven for the Silver Tassie; Genevieve Leaper for my own portrait; Les Byers of Ellisland Farm; Professor David Purdie for a most entertaining tour of Canongate Churchyard and Burns locations in Edinburgh; Pete Murray of Celtic Chords in Stonehaven for the loan of the fiddle for 'Rattlin, Roarin Willie'; Mrs Robertson for allowing me access to her land in Alloway to photograph the Brig o' Doon; Rev Gordon Farquharson; Iain McFadden; Tracy and Steven Singer of Brawliemuir; Calum Campbell; Ian Young; Brian Mahler; Lairhillock Inn near Stonehaven; and Aberdeen Art Gallery and Museums.

My thanks also go to Shirley Bell, Chief Executive of the Robert Burns World Federation for her willingness to facilitate communications with several of the contributors, and for her enthusiasm for the idea.

I would like to acknowledge the role of my friends at Mercat Press, now part of Birlinn Ltd, particularly Seán Costello and Tom Johnstone, who have encouraged me, challenged me and contained me with charm and skill over the course of the project. I have greatly valued your perceptiveness, creativity and friendship over the years.

My love and grateful thanks go to my wife, Sylvia, for her creative insight and continued support in allowing me to follow my photographic dreams. And to my son and daughter, Stuart and Lynsey, for sharing their thoughts, ideas and enthusiasm with me.

My final thanks go to my dear friends in the Stonehaven (Fatherland) Burns Club, of which I'm proud and privileged to be the current President. They have tracked this idea since its inception, and have given me encouragement every step of the way.

Index of Contributors